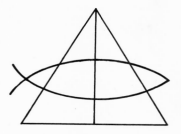

An
ARCHAEOLOGIST
looks
at the
GOSPELS

James L. Kelso

WORD BOOKS, Publishers

Waco, Texas • London, England

To the memory of
Miriam Adelphine Kelso

FOREWORD

The word "archaeology" usually suggests a field of study designed to shed light on the history, background, and customs which illuminate the study of the Old Testament.

Here, however, an archaeologist of genuine competence— acquired by more than forty years of research, archaeological field experience, and teaching—turns the spotlight on the historical and environmental factors reflected in the Gospels. The result is a highly interesting, easily readable account of first-century life which lies behind the gospel story.

The book is written for laymen. Hence, the apparatus of critical scholarship and the usual technicalities of archaeological works are not included.

Readers of this work will acquire a new grasp of Jesus as a genuine historical figure and a reverent insight into the setting into which our Lord came when He was "born in the likeness of men."

DONALD G. MILLER
Pittsburgh, Penna.

PREFACE

Whenever a professional archaeologist turns to a careful detailed study of the Gospels, only one thing dominates all his thinking. This is Jesus Christ himself. The personality of the Christ is unique and alone in all of human history. The archaeologist realizes more than anyone else the difference between B.C. and A.D.

With Christ, the archaeologist for the first time can understand the natural world, history, and man himself. Most important of all—God is now revealed so uniquely in Christ that man can no longer have any intellectual concept of deity which has not already been demonstrated in Jesus the Christ.

Therefore, in this volume the major emphasis is on Christ himself. The normal factors of archaeological interest, such as geography, history, architecture, commerce, literature, the arts and sciences, etc., will play a less important part in this book than in my former ones which dealt with the Old Testament.

JAMES L. KELSO
Pittsburgh, Penna.

CONTENTS

AN ARCHAEOLOGIST LOOKS AT THE GOSPELS

I

Bethlehem and the God
of War

THE ARCHAEOLOGIST'S first interest in any problem is geography, for his initial task is to separate mythology from history. He wants to know where a city or town was located, and what actually happened there.

Bethlehem, where the story of Jesus the Christ begins, is no mythological city but a real and historic one. It is referred to in eleven books of the Old Testament covering history from the Patriarchs to Nehemiah. It is mentioned as early as the 14th century B.C. in the Egyptian diplomatic correspondence found in the Tell Amarna Tablets.

Bethlehem was originally a city of the Canaanites dedicated to their god of war. The city's name means "the sanctuary city of Lahum," who was the Canaanite god of war. It was indeed an act of divine providence that the Prince of Peace was born in a sanctuary formerly dedicated to the god of war! After the conquest of Palestine the Jews revocalized the blasphemous name "Lahum" to make it read "lehem," which means "bread." In this way they gave Bethlehem a new name: "the house of bread." That title is also significant in the Christian story, for Jesus who was born here later identified himself as "the Bread of Life."

But the god of war that we meet in the Gospels is no longer Lahum. He has changed his name to Mars and is now the Roman god of war. The longest and bloodiest civil war in Rome's history finally ended with Augustus Caesar as emperor, and it was under his emperorship that Christ was born in far-off Bethlehem. Palestine had first been drawn into the war when the Roman general Pompey conquered Syria and Palestine in 63 B.C. Soon Pompey and Julius Caesar were fighting with one another for world empire, and both were using Jewish allies in the Near East. When Julius Caesar won, he came up to Palestine from his Egyptian victory to reward his Jewish backers. He made Antipater, the father of Herod the Great, procurator of Judea. In addition, he granted religious freedom to all the Jews in the empire, and he also released Jews from military service. The Jews showed their appreciation of this by being the most sincere mourners at the funeral of Julius Caesar.

His death, however, threw Palestine into new troubles, for Cassius, one of the new challengers for power, needed money desperately, and he imposed a heavy tribute on Antipater. But Cassius and Brutus were defeated at Philippi, and Asia became the dominion of Mark Anthony. Earlier Herod and Mark Anthony had been companions in the army, and Herod now prospered from that friendship. The great fortress which Herod built to defend his new Temple in Jerusalem was named Antonia in honor of their friendship. Meanwhile the Parthians, the new rulers of the old Persian homeland, suddenly swept over Syria and Palestine. Herod the Great fled before the Parthians and went to Petra and later to Rome. Here he was declared King of Judea, and with the aid of Anthony's army friends in Syria Herod conquered his new kingdom of Judea.

Herod now wanted to help his old friend Anthony in his fight against Octavius, who was later to take the title of Augustus. Fortunately for him, however, Cleopatra forced Herod to fight Arabia instead; and after the death of Anthony and Cleopatra, Augustus Caesar confirmed Herod in his kingdom and even extended his territorial boundaries.

During these civil wars, Palestine had within her borders military men from as far off as Britain in the west and from the Himalaya Mountains in the east. Rome had been bled white by this slaughter over who should be emperor, and military captives were so numerous that they could not even be sold economically as slaves. It was into this world that Jesus Christ was born as the Prince of Peace, when Mary and Joseph came to Bethlehem to report to the census takers in accordance with the edict of Augustus Caesar.[1]

But the god Mars refused to accept Jesus as his new rival. Herod the Great ordered the massacre of all the boy babies under two years of age in the Bethlehem area. It is most likely that his orders were carried out by soldiers from Herodium, one of his brilliant new cities with its key fortress towering above it. It lay just east across the valley from Bethlehem. This massacre of the infants was an easy order for Herod. He was a man without a conscience, among whose many victims were his favorite wife Mariamne and three of his own sons! One of these sons he killed shortly after the massacre of the innocents in Bethlehem. The two-year age limit set for the boys was probably similar to the modern Arabic custom in which the child is called two years old after his first birthday. If so, then the maximum age of the children killed was probably fourteen or fifteen months rather than twenty-four months.

The problem of the inn is still unsolved. We do not know what Palestinian inns were like. In the Roman empire, however, most inns were of bad repute, and travelers, whenever possible, stayed with friends or friends of friends they knew. Jewish inns may have had a better reputation, but this is only a conjecture. Other scholars think the word "inn" should be translated "caravansary," but again

---

[1] Luke 2:1–5.

we have no specific data on caravansaries. A third translation is the "guest house" of the city, as this word is also used of the "room" where the Last Supper was held. We simply do not know the exact character of the place where Christ was born.

No careful excavations have been carried on anywhere in Bethlehem except at the Church of the Nativity. This church, however, may well be located upon the site of the birthplace of Christ. Holy places were always significant to the people of the Old Testament, and many sites have remained holy to this day through the two-millenium epoch of the Christian Church and Mohammedanism. The people closely associated with the Christ would naturally carry on this Old Testament tradition of holy places. Furthermore, this Church of the Nativity was built before secular or church history had introduced any complicating problems.

The earliest nonscriptural reference to the birth of Christ is found in Justin Martyr, one of the early Church fathers, and is dated about A.D. 140. Justin Martyr stated that Christ was born in a cave. Origen said the same in A.D. 248. Later, Jerome, who was one of the most brilliant scholars of the early Church, gave us more details about this cave. Jerome's knowledge of all religious features in the neighborhood of Bethlehem was quite exact. In making his great Vulgate translation of the Scriptures he even used manuscripts from the same caves that gave us the Dead Sea Scrolls.

After the destruction of Jerusalem by the emperor Hadrian in A.D. 135, Jews were expelled from Bethlehem as from nearly all of Palestine. The sites most sacred to Jews and Christians were rededicated to Roman deities. This was done in Jerusalem on the site of the old Temple and also on the site of the crucifixion of Christ. Jerome tells us that the cave in which Christ was born was made a shrine to Adonis, one of the lovers of Venus, who was killed while he was hunting wild boar. This was simply the Greek version of the Tammuz myth of the Canaanites.

18

Right: *Church of the Nativity.*

Middle: *Interior of the Church of the Nativity.*

Bottom: *In this cave near Bethlehem, 85 Arab refugees lived at one time.*

Desert travel.

Below: *Traditional site of the shepherd's field near Bethlehem.*

Bottom: *Excavations at Herodium.*

It is from these two early Church fathers, both trustworthy scholars, that we get our tradition of Christ's birth in a cave. When Constantine became emperor of Rome he accepted Christianity and promoted the building of churches at the expense of the state. He and his mother Helena were especially interested in building churches on the most important sites of the life of Christ. This included both Jerusalem and Bethlehem. The work on the Church of the Nativity probably began in A.D. 325 when the empress Helena made a pilgrimage from Constantinople to Bethlehem.

The Church of the Nativity consisted of two units. The first was an octagonal structure immediately above and giving access to the cave. The second part of the church, used by the congregation, was a basilica opening off the octagonal unit and built to the west of it.

There is historical and archaeological evidence that this church may have been burned in the Samaritan revolt of A.D. 529. We do know for certain that about A.D. 530 Justinian ordered the demolition of the old church and the erection of a new basilica type church. This is the church that the visitor sees today, although numerous features of the building have been modified since the time of Justinian.

Americans tend to be puzzled at the thought of having a stable in a cave, but in antiquity the cave often made a good house, and in much of the world today, including Palestine, it still does. When the cave was demoted from being a house, it became a stable, and in Palestine it often serves that same use today as it did in Christ's time. Some older Arab houses still have a lower level unit in which the animals are kept in winter while the family lives on a higher level. The manger would likely be either a hollowed-out place in the wall of the cave or a large hollowed stone such as are often found in limestone districts. A wooden manger would be an expensive item, and no wooden ones are used today.

21

II

Shepherds and Magi

AMERICANS normally build their historical studies upon a chronological pattern, starting at the beginning of a man's life with the date of his birth. But when we come to study the life of Christ, the archaeologist has trouble at once identifying the exact year of his birth. The latest possible date for the birth of Christ is 4 B.C., since Herod the Great, who ordered the death of the boy babies in Bethlehem, died in the middle of March of that year.[1] In that spring we must allow forty days for Mary's purification[2] before she goes to the Temple and also time for the visit of the Magi.[3] Thus January of 4 B.C is the latest possible date for the birth of Christ.

The next information is that Christ was *about* thirty years of age when he began his ministry.[4] Most scholars put the beginning of the ministry in A.D. 27 or A.D. 28. That would put the birth of Jesus somewhere between 4 B.C. and 7 B.C. If Jewish arithmetic was used, then the dates would be one year less. The reference to Quirinius does not give us a specific date. All we know from histori-

---

[1] Matt. 2:16–19.   [2] Luke 2:22.   [3] Matt. 2:1–12.
[4] Luke 3:23. See Bruce M. Metzger, *The New Testament, Its Background, Growth, and Content* (New York: Abingdon Press, 1965), p. 104.

cal sources is that his second census was A.D. 7. If we assume the same fourteen-year interval that was later used in census taking, then Christ might have been born as early as 7 B.C.

The month of Jesus' birth is not specifically mentioned. Some scholars arrive at December by the following evidence. The priestly course to which the father of John the Baptist belonged served in the Temple in April and October. If we take the October date for the angel's initial visit to Zechariah, then the birth of John might have been in June. Since John was six months older than Jesus, Jesus could have been born in December.

The descriptive narrative of the nativity favors the months of December and January, since these months have the heaviest rains.[5] Bethlehem is located on the great north-south ridge road between Hebron and Jerusalem. The land to the west of Bethlehem is the higher and receives enough rain for farming. To the east there is only a narrow band of farmland before the land drops off quickly, falling away to the Dead Sea. Indeed, the eastern horizon of Bethlehem is the great land mass of Moab rising precipitously out of the Dead Sea chasm.

It is the shepherd who takes over the land east of Bethlehem in the great Judean wilderness. It was so in the days of David, who ran his flocks as far north as the city of Jericho and as far south as the oasis of Engedi on the Dead Sea. He also shepherded the plateaus east of Hebron, and his detailed knowledge of this whole territory enabled him to escape Saul's pursuit. In the days of the nativity Bethlehem shepherds used the same area; and today the Ta'amirieh Bedouin graze their sheep there. It was while shepherding flocks here that one of the Bedouin boys discovered the cave where the Dead Sea Scrolls were found.

The best season for the shepherds of Bethlehem is the winter when heavy rains bring up a luscious crop of new grass. After the rains the once-barren, brown desert earth

---

[5] In some years November has these same heavy rains.

is suddenly a field of brilliant green. One year when excavating at New Testament Jericho, I lived in Jerusalem and drove through this area twice every day. At one single point along the road, I could see at times as many as five shepherds with their flocks on one hillside. One shepherd stayed with his flock at the same point for three weeks, so lush was the grass. But as soon as the rains stopped in the spring, the land quickly took on its normal desert look once again.

Since there seem to have been a number of shepherds who came to see the Christ child, December or January would be the most likely months. If we are correct in putting the birth of Jesus in the winter season when good and bad weather tend to alternate, then the three- or four-day trip of Joseph and Mary to Bethlehem, or at least a part of it, may well have been during heavy rains. Some of these winter storms are best described in the Biblical phrase, "the heavens opened and the floods descended."

There seems to be no clue to the day of the month of his birth. The fourth-century church celebrated January 6th. December 25th was used in the ninth century.

When Jesus was born he was "wrapped in swaddling clothes."[6] The normal custom was to bathe the newborn infant in olive oil and rub in some salt.[7] Then the baby's arms were laid by his side and he was wrapped round and round with swaddling bands. One can see the babies so wrapped in some of the villages in Transjordan today. We do not know how long Joseph and Mary stayed in Bethlehem, but it seems to have been a minimum of a month and a half. At the end of eight days Jesus was circumcised. When he was forty days old, he was presented to the Lord in the Temple in Jerusalem at the time of Mary's purification according to the law of Moses.[8]

The next episode of interest to the archaeologist is the visit of the Magi (translated "wise men" in the RSV), but there is no chronology mentioned here except that Herod

---

[6] Luke 2:12.   [7] Ezek. 16:4.   [8] Luke 2:21–24.

the Great was still king. By the time of the birth of Jesus the term Magi had a variety of meanings both good and bad. The Magi were originally Iranian polytheists. But they had blended their old faith with Babylonian astrology and modern Greek philosophy. These particular Magi seemed to have emphasized the astrology factor, for they were interested in a unique star. (Astronomers argue as to what this phenomenon was, but they come to no common conclusion. There was, however, a conjunction of Jupiter and Saturn in the Pisces Constellation in 7 B.C. According to astrology, that meant "the ruler of the end of the world would come that year.")

We have no way of telling how much Old Testament knowledge these Magi had. They seemed to have been aware of a unique future king—an idea which they could have learned from the Jews living in their country; but the Magi had no detailed information as to where this king was to be born. They wisely came via Jerusalem to ask the Biblical scholars there the exact city where the new king was to be born. When Herod heard the story of these men, he urged them to find the child and report back to him. They continued on to Bethlehem where the star rested over the abode where Jesus was. No details are given as to the exact spot, but it was probably not the inn. When the enrollment at Bethlehem was concluded, Joseph would have had no trouble in finding a house—either living with relatives or renting rooms.

The Magi paid royal homage to the Christ and offered him appropriate gifts: gold, frankincense, and myrrh.[9] Matthew simply speaks of these Magi as being from the East, a most indefinite geographic term. Some scholars think these Magi were from Arabia since these gifts are Arabia's most important articles of commerce. Justin Martyr takes this interpretation as early as A.D. 140. The gifts, however, were among the most normal luxury items of the time and could have been bought in any country.

---

[9] Matt. 2:11.

25

Furthermore, if the Magi were coming from Arabia they would have passed through Bethlehem before coming to Jerusalem. Since the star is the key feature of their trip, it seems more likely they were from the area around old Babylon where astrology was treated as a science.

Artists today normally depict the Magi as riding on camels, and this is probably correct. The dromedary, a special breed of camel, furnished the fastest travel available. A good dromedary on a long journey could travel seventy miles a day—a distance far beyond the capabilities of a horse.

Arabia was a major source of gold in antiquity, and geologists working in that country today find many old abandoned gold mines. Frankincense is a fragrant gum resin which was used as incense in most of the religions in antiquity. It is milky white exudation from certain small trees in the Hadramaut district along the southern coast of Arabia. It is also grown in Punt (Ethiopia) in nearby Africa.

The Bible knows two varieties of myrrh. One is from the Gilead area of Palestine; the other came from the same Arabian area as frankincense. Myrrh is an aromatic resin but is also sold in liquid form as perfume. Persian kings wore myrrh in their crowns. Both frankincense and myrrh were used in the Temple ritual and were thus especially symbolic of him whose death did away with the whole sacrificial system. Just as myrrh was a gift at the birth of Christ, it was also offered to him at his death. At the crucifixion he was given "wine mingled with myrrh" as a painkiller, but he refused it. Myrrh was also one of the "spices" brought by Nicodemus for the burial rites of Christ.[10]

Herod had asked the Magi to report back to him, but "being warned in a dream not to return to Herod, they departed to their own country by another way."[11] This probably means that the Bethlehem shepherds took them

---

[10] Mark 15:23; John 19:39.   [11] Matt. 2:12.

over a secluded route through the wilderness of Judea either to the north or to the south of the Dead Sea. Then via Transjordan they could return to their homeland.

"Now when they had departed, behold, an angel of the Lord appeared to Joseph in a dream and said, 'Rise, take the child and his mother, and flee to Egypt, and remain there till I tell you; for Herod is about to search for the child, to destroy him.' "[12] The present Ta'amirieh Bedouin of Bethlehem often carry contraband between Jerusalem and Egypt, for they know all the smugglers' trails of the wilderness. Joseph's relatives in Bethlehem doubtless used these same desert trails until they came to Egypt. Here they would be safely out of Herod's jurisdiction, for Egypt was the property of Emperor Augustus himself.

At some indefinite time after the death of Herod the Great, Joseph was again told in a dream[13] to return to the land of Israel, " 'For those who sought the child's life are dead.' And he rose and took the child and his mother, and went to the land of Israel. But when he heard that Archelaus reigned over Judea in place of his father Herod, he was afraid to go there, and being warned in a dream he withdrew to the district of Galilee. And he went and dwelt in a city called Nazareth. . . ."[14]

---

[12] Matt. 2:13.

[13] If you are interested in knowing the modern Christian Arab's attitude about dreams, see Eric F. F. Bishop, *Jesus of Palestine* (London: Lutterworth Press, 1955), pp. 32ff.

[14] Matt. 2:20–23.

III

Samaritans and Essenes

THE SAMARITANS

THE SAMARITANS are usually assumed to be the descendants of intermarriage between the Israelites of the Northern Kingdom and foreign colonists brought into the land by the conquering Assyrians in 721 B.C. But actually Samaritan theology has no reflection of any of the religions brought in by the colonists. Indeed, it was A.D. 300 before the Jewish rabbis officially declared the Samaritans to be heretics.

The major schism between the Jews and the Samaritans occurred when the Samaritans built their own temple on Mt. Gerizim, probably in the days of Ezra. Shechem at the base of that mountain then became their sacred city, but Samaria remained the political capital until the days of Alexander the Great. Alexander appointed one of his generals as governor of Samaria, but this man was assassinated by some of the Samaritan leaders. After that experience the city was for Greeks only, and Shechem became the Samaritan capital as well as holy city. The Samaritan temple was destroyed by John Hyrcanus in 121 B.C. Many of the Samaritans then used the Jerusalem Temple. In New Testament times, Samaritan synagogues, like Jewish ones, were scattered around the Mediterranean Sea at key points of the trade routes.

The Samaritan canon included only the first five books of the Old Testament, and they read a different text in Deuteronomy which ordered a temple to be built on Mt. Gerizim. The remains of that temple may well be found under the Roman temple built by the emperor Hadrian. Excavations are now going on at this site. In Christ's time the Pharisees rated the Samaritans with the Sadducees, for both of these groups rejected the doctrine of the resurrection as taught by the Pharisees.

Among the common people there was little love lost between Jews and Samaritans. This was demonstrated when Jesus asked the Samaritan woman for a drink and she replied, " 'How is it that you, a Jew, ask a drink of me, a woman of Samaria?' For Jews have no dealings with Samaritans."[1] One Samaritan village refused to entertain Jesus.[2] And one of the insults the Jews heaped on Jesus was to call him "a Samaritan" and "one who has a demon."[3]

Jesus himself considered the Samaritans to be ceremonially clean, for he drank from their vessels, ate their food, and slept in their homes. Furthermore he treated this Samaritan woman as a true Jewess, and she and many other Samaritans accepted Jesus as the Messiah. Jesus, however, did reject her view that Mt. Gerizim was the true sanctuary. He insisted that it was Jerusalem. Then he added, "Woman, believe me, the hour is coming when neither on this mountain nor in Jerusalem will you worship the Father. . . . But the hour is coming, and now is, when the true worshipers will worship the Father in spirit and truth, for such the Father seeks to worship him."[4]

Christ also speaks well of Samaritans in other places. In one of His parables a priest and a Levite traveling the Jericho road passed by a Jew who was beaten by robbers, but they gave him no help. It was a Samaritan who cared for the injured man, took him to an inn, and paid his bill.[5] Ten lepers were healed, but the only one who returned to

[1] John 4:9. [2] Luke 9:51-56. [3] John 8:48. [4] John 4:21-23.
[5] Luke 10:29-37.

29

thank Jesus was a Samaritan.[6] In Christ's plan for world evangelism the Samaritan was a special object of his care, and the early church carried out this commission.[7]

THE ESSENES

The Dead Sea Scrolls have made many contributions to the study of the Gospels, although most of these contrast the relationship between the teachings of the Essenes and the Gospels. But first a word of history on the Essenes.

The Essenes originated with a super-orthodox group of Jewish priests from the old high priestly family of Zadok. They were horrified by the action of the Maccabees who had usurped the high priesthood and then the Davidic kingship. These dissenters abandoned Jerusalem and its Temple. They went down to the desert neighborhood of the Dead Sea to wait for God to work some miracle for them as he had done for Israel at Sinai. When no miracle came, they formed themselves into a new Jewish sect with their own theology, their own song book, and their own church government. Secular history of the Jews knew them as the Essenes.

These men thought of themselves as the true preservers of the Old Testament Scriptures and traditions. They sought to preserve both by different but still more difficult regulations than those laid down by the Pharisees. Their headquarters were a sort of monastery complex at Qumran. Those who sought membership in the group lived in tents and caves around the monastery. In each small group there was always a member busy at Bible study every hour of the day. They emphasized continued purification by successive lustrations, and they had their own super-orthodox regulations for all phases of life.

The entrance requirements and monastery rules of the Essenes were very demanding and difficult to fulfill, so that comparatively few Jews joined their ranks. Some of their members lived outside the Qumran area either as individu-

---

[6] Luke 17:16.   [7] Acts 1:8; 8:1–25.

Samaritan priests with the scroll of their Bible— the Pentateuch.

Jacob's well today is covered by an unfinished Orthodox church.

Above: *Qumran, headquarters of the Essenes with the Dead Sea in the background. The caves where the scrolls were hidden are some distance away.* Below: *Cave 4 at Qumran, showing windows opening into the cave.*

als or in small groups, but everything of importance was centered in Qumran. The Essenes made little impression on the common people among whom Christ centered his ministry. Only occasionally did Christ touch upon their eccentric doctrines. He objected to their attitude toward the Sabbath, which was far stricter than that of the Pharisees. He also strongly refuted their doctrine of hatred, for the Essenes actually *taught hatred* toward all men who were not truly godly as they themselves defined the term.[8]

The Essenes had an initial baptism into membership and a communal meal, but the former was totally unlike Christian baptism and the latter was in no way related to the Lord's Supper. The Essenes called themselves "the new covenant," for this was in contrast to the "false covenant" of the Jerusalem Temple theologians whom they hated. But their "new covenant" was in no way related to the new covenant of Scripture. They also called themselves "the elect"—which is a Petrine and a Pauline term—and they considered themselves "sons of light"—a Johannine and a Pauline term. Neither Essene designation was similar to the New Testament term. The whole Essene concept of the Messiah was wrong. They actually had *two* Messiahs.[9] They had no doctrine of original sin, no Calvary, no offer of salvation to all men, and no resurrection as the New Testament knows it.

The major heresy of the Essenes was to make God the Creator of good and *evil* spirits. This heresy permeates all their theology. It was an Iranian heresy which some of these Jews had brought back from Mesopotamia. To the Essenes, good men were under the influence of good spirits and wicked men were under the influence of evil spirits. They were constantly talking of good and evil, light and darkness, truth and falsehood, but in the heresy pattern of the Iranian mythology and in direct opposition to the

---

[8] See chapter VIII for further discussion of this point.
[9] This will be discussed further in chapter VI.

teaching of both the Old Testament and the New Testament as it later developed.

The Apostle John often used the same vocabulary as the Essenes but always in an entirely different sense. He emphasized Christ's remark, "I am the light of the world; he who follows me will not walk in darkness, but will have the light of life."[10] Notice also how John begins his Gospel. It is a direct refutation of everything that is Essene. "In the beginning was the Word, and the Word was with God, and the Word was God. He was in the beginning with God; all things were made through him, and without him was not anything made that was made. In him was life, and the life was the light of men. The light shines in the darkness, and the darkness has not overcome it."[11]

There is, however, one very constructive contribution that the Dead Sea Scrolls have made. The Old Testament manuscripts that were found among the Scrolls show a text about 900 years older than any known up to that discovery. Therefore, Old Testament references to the Messiah can now be checked back to the time of Christ himself or even a century earlier. The canon of the Old Testament used by the Essenes seems to have been the same as that of the Pharisees—which is identical with that of modern Judaism and Protestantism. As a result of non-biblical material found in the Dead Sea Scrolls, we now know that all of the books of the New Testament could easily have been written before A.D. 85. Most of them were doubtless finished before Jerusalem was destroyed in A.D. 70.

One of the finds in Cave One was a complete manuscript of Isaiah which was written at least 150 years before Christ began his ministry. This manuscript has a most interesting textual history, as its ancestry goes back to the Babylonian Exile. We know exactly what the scroll of Isaiah looked like from which Christ read the lesson in the Nazareth synagogue shortly after his baptism. (Inciden-

---

[10] John 8:12.   [11] John 1:1–5.

tally, Isaiah was one of the Essenes' favorite books of Scripture.)

This Dead Sea Scroll was a leather manuscript made of seventeen skins all prepared very carefully and sewed together into a long roll. The scroll was 23¾ feet long and 10¼ inches wide. There are fifty-four columns of writing in the scroll and its clear black ink can easily be read today.

IV

Jesus' Boyhood

SINCE Mary brought only turtledoves or pigeons as her sacrificial offering at her purification service in the Jerusalem Temple after the birth of Jesus, it is only natural to assume that the family was poor rather than middle-class or rich.[1] If this economic theory is correct, then the home of Joseph and Mary was most likely only a one-room or at the most a two-room house. An additional room would have been needed to serve as the carpenter shop. It would have been located alongside of the living quarters rather than below them, as Nazareth was only a small town. We shall describe the typical house of a poor family as the archaeologist finds it when he digs up a New Testament city.

The poor of Palestine have always lived out of doors when the weather permits. The kitchen, then as now, was in the open air immediately in front of the house. There would be an oven here for baking bread, although there might also be a second oven in one corner of the house for winter weather. The importance of these little ovens to the people cannot be overemphasized. They supplied approximately three-fourths of the food of the poor. In the Lord's Prayer, "bread" is the word for "food," and the

---

[1] Luke 2:24; compare Lev. 12:8.

prayer is phrased for the poor man—"one day's bread at a time." Most of the work of the day was carried on in this yard if weather permitted, and it also served as a patio where friends would be entertained.

Just as the front yard served as an extra room, the same was true of the roof. It was a bedroom during the hot nights. It served for the drying of grapes and figs, etc., for winter use. It might even be a summer storeroom.

In the winter the one-room house served as kitchen, living room, and bedroom. Here the family also stored as large a supply of foodstuffs as could be afforded, especially grains and olive oil. The family clothes were stored in chests, and the tools of the trade of the owner had to be kept here as well. Even the farmer's plow and other equipment were stored in the room—a room which might be even less than nine by twelve feet. Fortunately, the people of Palestine were small of stature! From this description of the one- or two-room house such as Jesus probably grew up in, you can see that what we call poverty in America today would have been luxury in the eyes of the New Testament poor.

Much of Jesus' boyhood would have been centered around the "carpenter shop." The Hebrew ancestor of the word "carpenter" is best translated "skilled craftsman" and refers to workers in wood, stone, and metal. A better translation than carpenter for the Gospel term is "woodworker," for the work done by Joseph and Jesus is not what we commonly think of as carpenter work. No Palestinian built a house of wood as we do. Assuming that Jesus was a craftsman working in wood, what were the various tasks he carried out?

There were no sawmills, so the men who worked in wood had to make their own lumber. This meant felling the trees, transporting the logs to the workshop, ripsawing the logs to get lumber, and drying it so as to avoid warping. This handling of logs and green lumber was manual labor that called for brute strength. It would account at least in part for the magnificent physique that Jesus demonstrated through the years of his ministry. Arab stevedores today carry loads of 400 and 500 pounds. When I asked an Arab physician what was the heaviest load he had ever known a man to carry, he replied, "Nine hundred pounds."

The making of lumber also required careful skill. To appreciate the kind of skill, sometime try ripsawing a log, keeping the boards always of the same thickness! Different varieties of trees had to be cut down and their lumber kept in store, for only certain woods are best for specific articles. Holm oak, for example, makes the best plows. Sycamore is useful for cheap furniture and coffins or roof beams. Oak is the best hardwood for most purposes. Olive wood takes a beautiful finish and was used by Solomon for the carved cherubim in the Temple. Cedar from the Lebanons was the most prized wood in the Near East.

If Jesus worked in the full range of a craftsman in wood, then he was engaged in at least the following tasks. For the farmer he made plows, yokes, threshing sledges, pitchforks, shovels for winnowing, and ox goads. For the builder he made doors and lattice windows, furnished the roof logs and usually put them in place. He also made any furniture that was used in the house—bed, stool, lampstand, table, and chest for holding bedding and clothes.

He was also a cabinetmaker, selling his skill, no doubt, to the wealthy of nearby Sepphoris. Give an Arab cabinetmaker today a furniture catalogue and he can reproduce any kind of furniture you wish and do it with only half a dozen tools.

Nazareth was in a forested area just far enough away from Sepphoris so that Joseph and Jesus could find plenty of trees to fell, but close enough to the capital to give them an excellent market for the finished product. Nazareth, although only a small town, was at the junction of seven crossroads just three miles south of Sepphoris. This latter city had been a rabid Jewish community, and at the death of Herod the Great, it gave the Romans so much trouble that they burned the city and sold its inhabitants as slaves. Then Herod Antipas rebuilt the city with an emphasis on Graeco-Roman culture after the architectural style of his father Herod the Great. During all the boyhood of Jesus and through much of his early manhood, Sepphoris remained the capital of Galilee.

The boy Jesus learned his trade from Joseph.[2] You can see the same family relationship today in Bethlehem where the olive wood workers are busy at their trade. Some of these small boys are already highly skillful at the inlay work. Finally remember that Jesus, the boy who worked in wood, must die as a man on a "tree."

While we are on the subject of Jesus' boyhood, we shall take the arbitrary date of twelve years as the approximate conclusion of his boyhood. Twelve years and a day is set by the Mishnah[3] for manhood. An extreme date for Jewish boyhood would be fifteen years. Death came early in the ancient world!

But Jesus had other tasks besides shop work. While quite young he probably took his turn looking after the sheep of his family and those of his neighbors. His shepherd passages are too exact and meaningful to be hearsay. The shepherd boy knew the farmers' fields almost as well as the pasture lands, for he was permitted to graze his sheep *near* a farm but never on it until after the grain was harvested. Jesus doubtless helped at harvest time in the fields, for there were never enough hands to gather in the harvest of barley and wheat. He himself said, "The harvest is plentiful, but the laborers are few."[4] Early in life Jesus met the absentee landlord and his stewards along with the tax collectors who later appeared in his parables.

Jesus would also have assisted in gathering the grape and the olive crops. This section of Galilee was famous for its

---

[2] Joseph and Jesus are both spoken of as carpenters—the former in Matt. 13:55 and the latter in Mark 6:3.

[3] The Mishnah is the traditional doctrine of the Jew as represented by the rabbinic decisions before the third century A.D.

[4] Matt. 9:37.

olives. For these tasks he might be paid in kind, or more likely Joseph was paid in kind for Jesus' work. Note all the allusions to food items in the talks of Jesus—the grain and the mill that ground it, the yeast and the bread and the oven that baked it. All phases of grape culture are referred to. Figs and olives are there, and the spices used to diversify a common menu—mint, anise, mustard, cummin, etc.

As a shepherd Jesus would have learned almost everything about the great outdoors where he lived. For example, notice all the allusions made to weather (incidentally, many of these fine points do not show up in a translation). Watch the mention of plants and trees in his remarks.

Israelite history, too, was spread out before him when as a boy he took his sheep to the hilltop above Nazareth (the village lay on a hillside close to a good spring). To the west he could see the Mediterranean where Jonah had sailed when he failed to evangelize his enemies. Jesus must have learned early the meaning of loving enemies and evangelizing the world. Jonah's home town of Gath-hepher was only a couple of miles from Nazareth, so when Jesus talked of Jonah he was speaking of virtually another hometown boy. Cedar logs for all the temples built in Jerusalem's history came on rafts down those same Mediterranean waters.

Jesus could also see the Carmel headland jutting out into the Mediterranean. In Canaanite times it had made a perfect sanctuary for Baal, the god of vegetation, and Ashera, goddess of the sea. Here Elijah triumphed over the false priests of those wicked sanctuaries; and it was from Carmel that Elijah ran as a footman before Ahab all the way across the great Esdraelon plain. Jesus would recognize in Elijah the necessity of a servant of God having unique physical strength as well as outstanding spiritual power. No wonder the Old Testament prophets spoke of Elijah as the forerunner of the Messiah. And Jesus was to meet that same Elijah on another Galilean mountaintop.

It was in this same valley of Esdraelon that Deborah and

Barak had earlier defeated the Canaanite-Galilean military alliance. At that time, there was another heathen sanctuary close at hand, another Bethlehem. Indeed, the greatest of all the sanctuaries dedicated to the Canaanite god of war was less than ten miles from the home of Jesus. (The Bethlehem where Jesus was born had been a minor sanctuary of Lahum, the god of war.)

From his hilltop vantage point Jesus could see Mt. Gilboa where the wicked Saul fell in battle, and where, from those very same heights, faithful Gideon had earlier rushed down to defeat the enemies of Israel in the valley below. That was the same valley that Saul later traveled in order to visit with a witch the night before his death.

The family of Jesus went every year to the Passover at Jerusalem;[5] and Jesus walked through Israelite history all the way, not only Old Testament history, but also his nation's later experiences with Alexander the Great, the Ptolemies of Alexandria, the Seleucids of Antioch, the Parthians from Iran, and the Romans. These Jewish holidays remind us that there was another major field of study for the young Jesus besides nature and history—namely, the Bible of his day which we now call the Old Testament.

He studied his Bible at the synagogue school, and this is where his photographic memory was most valuable, for handwritten Bibles were so expensive that the only way to own a Bible was to write it on the tablets of your memory. And a phenomenal memory was a prerequisite for anyone who was to be a Bible scholar in those days. Not only did the Bible have to be memorized but also all the rabbinic teachings had to be memorized. At twelve years of age Jesus used his phenomenal memory as well as his brilliant mind to confound the Temple scholars in Jerusalem at the Passover season. His parents "found him in the temple, sitting among the teachers, listening to them and asking them questions; and all who heard him were amazed at his understanding and his answers."[6]

---

[5] Luke 2:41.   [6] Luke 2:46–47.

41

Every Christian should sit down and read through the Gospel of Matthew swiftly, noticing only the phenomenal breadth of Jesus' knowledge. Then you will realize that here was one who as a boy was already an intellectual genius interested in everything, and possessed of a photographic memory to preserve it.

Luke concludes the boyhood of Jesus with this summary: "And Jesus increased in wisdom and in stature, and in favor with God and man."[7] We have already stressed the early wisdom of Jesus, his physical prowess and his spiritual life; but note that Luke also stresses Jesus' unique ability to get along with *people*. The rest of the Gospel story demonstrates the accuracy of Luke's evaluation of Jesus' boyhood. The entire earthly life of Jesus the Christ is an expansion of Luke's summary of his boyhood.

---

[7] Luke 2:52.

*Harvesting olives,
a major crop
near Nazareth
in Christ's day.*

Nazareth today.

Mount of Precipitation (above) near Nazareth is traditionally considered the hill from which the townspeople tried to throw Jesus.

A street in Jerusalem (the old city).

Fragments from the Dead Sea Scrolls.

V

Christ's Early Manhood

LUKE SAYS that Jesus was about thirty years of age when he began his ministry.[1] Assuming a date for the birth of Christ at 5 B.C., then Christ would be twelve years old in A.D. 7, at the time when he reasoned with the rabbis in the Temple in Jerusalem. If we date the beginning of his ministry in A.D. 27 or A.D. 28, then there are some twenty silent years in the life of Christ.

Most people think of Christ as a young man, but in the chronology of those days the life span was so short that a Jewish boy could be legally married at thirteen years and a day, and a girl at twelve years and a day! While boys were more likely to marry somewhat later, i.e., between fifteen and eighteen, girls married shortly after the minimum legal age. Thus the women of Nazareth who were of the same age as Christ were all grandmothers, and at least a few of the boyhood chums of Jesus would have been grandfathers before Christ began his active ministry! So we must realize that Christ was decidedly a mature man in the eyes of his fellow Jews when he left Nazareth to begin his work.

The early manhood of Jesus was certainly the most important of all the years of the preparation for his ministry. As a boy he had mastered his trade of woodworking, and

[1] Luke 3:23.

45

was then able to concentrate on "the world of ideas" during the hours while he worked at his craft. His sermons demonstrate the phenomenal breadth and maturity of his learning. His visits at Sepphoris constantly put him in a major center of business and politics. Here he picked up a wealth of source material which he fashioned into his parables. Here he heard thousands of proverbs, those pithy phrases used to clinch any argument—political, social, economic, or religious. Today a missionary to the Arabs should know about 5000 parables and have them at his tongue's end for instant use. Sepphoris had plenty of Greek culture, too, for Christ to study. Its large Greek theatre is an indication of the high place Greek influence had in this capital city. Herod Antipas did not move his capital from Sepphoris to Tiberius until about five or six years before Christ began his ministry.

Certainly Jesus continued the family custom of going every year to the Passover feast at Jerusalem. As a man he doubtless attended the other holy days at Jerusalem as he did during his ministry. In that city the Bible was the essence of his observation and desire. But to judge from his remarks in the Gospels he must have often been disappointed to discover that tradition was more important than Scripture among the leaders of his nation. Most important, at Jerusalem Jesus had contact with the finest Bible manuscripts such as were available at no other place.

Jesus was also a man of the great out-of-doors, and he constantly blended scientific observation with revealed theology. How happily he blended the two! "Follow me, and I will make you fishers of men."[2] "Behold, I send you out as sheep in the midst of wolves; so be wise as serpents and innocent as doves."[3] "Foxes have holes, and birds of the air have nests; but the Son of man has nowhere to lay his head."[4] "I am the good shepherd. The good shepherd lays down his life for the sheep."[5]

Luke mentioned in summarizing the youth of Jesus that he grew "in favor with God and man." This ability to mix

---

[2] Matt. 4:19. [3] Matt. 10:16. [4] Luke 9:58. [5] John 10:11.

46

with people must have followed him through manhood, for his whole ministry is a demonstration of how to influence people even when working with *all* kinds of folk. The disciples whom Jesus chose were strong men and needed a master hand at the helm! Remember that they would later turn the world upside down. Even his enemies, the Pharisees, could not resist his personality, and again and again they came back to argue with him. They even invited him into the super-kosher sanctuary of their homes.

Through the years of early manhood Jesus also grew in favor with God. In the Gospels we are shown those silent watches in the night, those times apart by day. These secret times with the Father were not new experiences in his ministry. They were simply the climax of earlier years of like experiences. Here in the secret hours in the Father's presence the most important of all his experiences transpired which prepared him for his active ministry. Here is where he found revelation far beyond that of his beloved Bible. Here is where he must learn the *ultimate*, and he knew it. Once the Gospels were written they could not be revised! His disciples might not understand revelation as he talked with them, but he must phrase it so that new experiences would recall it to mind and produce not only the correct answer but also the compulsion that would demand obedience even at the cost of death. "He taught them as one who had authority, and not as their scribes."[6]

The teachings of Christ are of such a nature that we sense he must have meditated on them over and over again through the long years, and silently tested them against the experiences he met in city and village and along the dusty road. The compulsion of God was upon him, and that demanded perfection! *He must be already perfect before he begins his ministry.* He must also command his own disciples: "You, therefore, must be perfect, as your heavenly Father is perfect."[7]

One interesting feature strikes an archaeologist as he

---

[6] Matt. 7:29.   [7] Matt. 5:48.

reads the Gospels in a red-letter edition. Here Christ's words, printed in red, stand out prominently against their contextual background printed in black. These sayings of Christ (except in their allusions to the Old Testament) are so universal in statement and so timeless in their nature that the archaeologist does not find too much material to work on, except by way of their striking contrast with all other religious ideas of the ancient world. It is in the black letter text that the archaeologist finds the technical fields for his study.

VI

John the Baptist
and Christ's Temptation

THE FINDING of the Dead Sea Scrolls has naturally brought up the question of the relationship of John the Baptist to the Essene community at Qumran. Scholars are of two general groups. Some say that John was or may have been a member of that community at some time. Others deny that he was in any way related to them. One conclusion, however, is certain: When John the Baptist began teaching he had advanced infinitely beyond the teaching of the Essenes. John's *essential duty* was to point out the Messiah, but to that end he also was a great preacher and he won the crowds. Indeed, all classes of society came into the desert to hear him preach the repentance of sin. Furthermore, John was a brilliant teacher, for some of his disciples were later chosen by Christ himself for his own apostles. John fitted perfectly into the picture of the Old Testament prophets, but in no sense did he fit into the pattern of Essene doctrine and practice.

Although the Essenes were conscientious Bible students and some of them were at Bible study during each of the twenty-four hours of the day, nevertheless they had *missed* the whole Old Testament concept of the Messiah. They

49

actually looked for two Messiahs—the Messiah of Aaron and the Messiah of Israel. They looked for one to be a priestly Messiah and the other to be a political Messiah. And with the Essenes the Messiah from the tribe of Levi was to be superior to the Messiah from the tribe of Judah! Their conclusions are an excellent demonstration of inter-testamental theology, where human reason was made superior to the revelation of the Old Testament itself.

The Essenes invented this heresy in spite of the fact that they used an excellent Messianic text as the reason for their separation from the heretical Maccabean priesthood which had usurped the Jerusalem Temple. They used the same passage out of Isaiah[1] that John the Baptist was to use a century and a half later when he proclaimed himself to be "the voice of one crying out in the wilderness." But the Essenes interpreted "clearing the way of the Lord" not as Messianic but as studying the Mosaic law, and obeying it and other prophetic writings. Like the Sadducees and the Pharisees they were simply another group of legalists.

John the Baptist, on the other hand, was anything but a legalist. He was not a "relative" of Moses but of Elijah. He was anything else but a quiet "secret society" Essene teacher. Instead he was an outdoor evangelist shouting to the great crowds. He addressed both the laity and the clergy of Israel, and called both of them a "brood of vipers," fleeing "from the wrath to come," i.e., deadly serpents fleeing before an all-consuming prairie fire. John insisted that the only true mark of a son of Abraham was repentance, not legalism.[2] Furthermore, his unique work was to introduce the Messiah to these lost sheep of the house of Israel.

John's once-for-all baptism differs completely from the baptism plus multiple lustrations of the Essenes. The one thing that instantly stands out in Qumran is the intricate and ubiquitous water system. No other site in Palestine is like this one. And remember this water system is in the

---

[1] Isa. 40:3–5. [2] Matt. 3:7, 8; Luke 2:7, 8.

desert, secured from winter cloudbursts in the mountains, collected in great reservoirs! John, however, used only the old Jordan river, a few miles distant from Qumran, but sanctified by the experience of Joshua and his hosts at Jericho and by the heavenly exit of Elijah from these same waters.

These Essenes, in spite of their lustrations, never met their Messiah; but John the Baptist found Jesus, the true Messiah, here at the Jordan River, awaiting baptism and commanding it of John, in spite of the latter's sincere objection that Christ should baptize him rather than he baptize Christ. But in all this water baptism, John insisted that the real and the only effective baptism was to be the baptism of the Holy Spirit which only Christ the Messiah could give!

At the baptism of Christ we meet the Trinity for the first time—Father, Son, and Holy Spirit. In the Old Testament we meet God and his Messiah; but only very rarely is there a prediction of the Holy Spirit. In the Old Testament God is very much like the Father in the New Testament, although at other times in the Old Testament God is working as the Son or Holy Spirit did in the New Testament.

In the Gospels "the plans and specifications" of the Messiah in the Old Testament are fulfilled in the person and work of Jesus the Christ. With the "birthday" of the Holy Spirit on Pentecost and through the remainder of the New Testament we get the demonstration of the person and work of the Holy Spirit, i.e., that other Christ.

Archaeology finds absolutely nothing of the concept of the Trinity in any other religion in antiquity. There are "sets" of three gods, but they are normally father, mother, and son, or they are a synthesis of three gods into a common concept. Indeed, the absence of the *mother concept* in the whole idea of God in the Old Testament makes that faith unique in antiquity!

In fact, human reason today is powerless to philosophize on the Trinity as it was in Christ's day and in Paul's time. The Trinity is a matter of faith, not reason. Unfortunately, reason has been vastly overemphasized in our day at the expense of faith. Physically speaking, no person anywhere on earth knows *how* he digests his food and uses its energy for life's purposes. Yet, by faith we eat and by faith we utilize the products of eating. The essence of science is to learn, and *learning* is always an *unfinished* product! I graduated from pharmacy college as a young man, but science has moved so phenomenally rapidly since that time, that today very little remains of the "assured results of science" which I studied. The scientific method demands the finding of new data, and that compels the restudy of everything known to date.

But the Trinity is the same yesterday, today, and forever! Then and now, God the Father is everything that we know of God; the same is true of the Son and of the Holy Spirit. Yet, although each is the same, each is also different. We "know this by experience"—that is Paul's phrase—but we cannot explain it to non-Christians. Indeed, the summary of all Christian work is world evangelism, sealed by baptism "in the name of the Father and of the Son and of the Holy Spirit," and continuously teaching these converts to do all that Christ has commanded.[3]

After the baptism, "Jesus was led up by the Spirit into the wilderness to be tempted by the devil."[4] Whatever were the techniques which Satan used in the last two temptations of Christ, the archaeologist can at least see what the backgrounds of both temptations were.

When Christ was challenged to jump from the pinnacle of the Temple, the archaeologist is reminded that one of the architectural features of Herod's Temple at Jerusalem was height. The great retaining wall of the Temple courtyard area at the southeast corner towered 150 feet above the Kidron valley, and the topmost height of the sanctuary building itself was another 150 feet in height. Scholars differ as to whether "the pinnacle of the temple" refers to the southeast corner of the Temple courtyard or to the top

---

[3] Matt. 28:19–20.   [4] Matt. 4:1.

The wilderness of Judea where Christ was tempted.

The Jordan River near the Dead Sea.

The corner wall in the foreground may be the "pin-nacle of the Temple" referred to in the account of Christ's temptation. It was 150 ft. high in his day but is only half that high today.

The archaeological site of New Testament Jericho.

of the sanctuary building itself. The Greek term for "pinnacle" also means "edge," and the Greek term translated "temple" is normally used for the courtyard area of the Temple rather than for the sanctuary building itself; therefore, perhaps the 150 foot perpendicular wall at the southeast corner of the Temple courtyard is referred to. Furthermore, the top of the sanctuary building was apparently flat and without a pinnacle.

Satan also took Christ up into an exceeding high mountain and showed him all the kingdoms of the world and the glory of them. At this point the archaeologist is reminded that, if Christ during the forty days of temptation in the wilderness came at any time to the eastern edge of the high Judean mountain wilderness, he could have looked directly down on the New Testament city of Jericho. Here was a city where Herod the Great had *duplicated* as far as was possible the *city of Rome itself.* And Rome, of course, was *symbolic of the whole world!*

Herod the Great had gone to Rome to visit his patron the Emperor Augustus Caesar. While there he took a deep interest in the new city which the emperor was creating for Rome. When Herod returned to Palestine he took with him expert Roman architects and builders, and at New Testament Jericho he reproduced as far as possible a miniature Rome. Its architecture was of the "opus reticulatum" type which is best seen today by visiting the ruins of Pompeii. Along both banks of the Wadi Qelt, Herod the Great built for himself the brilliant winter capital of Jericho, giving it all the luxuries of a modern Miami.

Although it seldom freezes in Jerusalem, the city has a bitterly cold, damp winter climate. In Bible days the city's houses were practically unheated according to our definition of comfort. The people used only charcoal braziers. So the damp chill of Jerusalem gnawed at the bones of every citizen, and whoever could afford it went down to the glorious winter heat and sunshine of Jericho. Even the priests and Levites enjoyed this luxury whenever possible. So here in Herod's winter capital was a city unlike any

55

other in the world with the exception of Rome. Here was concentrated in Palestine a city typifying the world's kingdoms, by whose power and glory Satan tried to tempt Christ.

Then the devil left Christ, "and behold, angels came and ministered to him."[5]

[5] Matt. 4:11.

VII

Christ's Ministry in Capernaum

As a young professor of the Old Testament, I read all the books available in that field. Many of the authors on Old Testament interpretation spoke of the numerous discrepancies in the Bible. They even said that many of the events could not have happened. But when I actually visited the sites of these Bible stories in Palestine, and read the Bible on the very spot where the events took place, ninety percent of all these so-called scholarly problems disappeared! Therefore let us go at once to Tell Hum, the ruins of Capernaum, and study the Gospel narratives on the site where they happened.

Christ's ministry was not primarily in the big cities like Jerusalem, Caesarea, Samaria, Sepphoris and Jericho. His major work, except for Passion Week, was done in small cities and country towns. After his baptism and temptation Christ moved up to Galilee and made Capernaum the center of his labors. Tiberius, the brilliant new capital which had replaced Sepphoris, was just a few miles down the west shore of the Sea of Galilee. But Christ chose Capernaum. Here commerce from Transjordan crossed the Jordan river just before that stream entered the Sea of

Galilee. It was the border crossing between the territory of Herod Antipas and that of his brother Herod Philip. Thus both commerce and politics came through this narrow funnel and Christ's message could be ideally broadcast from there, but always with the intimate touch of a small city.

There were eight other small cities with a minimum population of 15,000 each scattered at various places around the Sea of Galilee. From these small cities and smaller towns Christ drew most of the disciples who would later evangelize the world. He would, of course, indirectly influence the life of some of the people of Tiberius, and others in the closer large commercial center of Magdala, which was busy salting fish for both Palestinian and foreign commerce.

Capernaum was also on a direct route from the Tetrarchy of Philip to Ptolemais, the major port of Galilee on the Mediterranean. And it had other advantages, for on both sides of the Sea of Galilee were very famous health resorts. The one near Tiberius is even mentioned by the Roman Pliny. Another one was less than two miles from Capernaum. As you read the Gospel narratives, it may seem that Christ healed more sick people than the population of Capernaum itself. But remember that all year long there was a steady stream of sick folk coming to these spas for better health. It was only a short distance from the health resorts to Capernaum where this new miracle worker was healing all kinds of diseases.

The Sea of Galilee is heart-shaped, about twelve miles long, and five miles at the widest point which is where Magdala is located on the western shore. The lake is about 600 feet below sea level. Although a small lake, it can be as treacherous as any sea when the sudden squalls churn up the water. I recall the story told by a professor of Greek who crossed the lake to visit the Greek cities on the Transjordan side, and whose boat was caught in one of the sudden cyclonic storms.[1] He said he would not have

---

[1] Cf. Matt. 8:24ff.

missed that boat ride for anything in the world, but that nothing would ever get him on that lake a second time.

Peter and Andrew, James and John were men who fished these waters daily, and they were he-men often battered by the storm. There is something magnificent about these strong men being the close followers of one who had a still stronger physique. James and John were especially brawny—Christ nicknamed them "sons of thunder." It was these men who wanted to call down fire from heaven, as Elijah did, upon the Samaritans who would not entertain Christ.[2]

Matthew, the tax collector, came from Capernaum.[3] This is the type of businessman the church of today must win—a man of the world who once worshiped the "almighty dollar" but now worships Christ and dedicates his business talent to world evangelism. Matthew was in charge of a major frontier custom house, a position that demanded that he be a master in both business and politics, and at the same time a social genius so as not to be ostracized as a tax collector. I have often wondered how Judas became the treasurer of the disciple group instead of Matthew who seemed so much better qualified.[4] Taxation in those days as now spared no one, and these fishermen disciples had doubtless paid a fishing tax to Matthew or one of his subordinates every working day.

Jesus was not only the master physician but also the superb teacher, equally at home with small groups in small towns or with mass evangelism of crowds of 4,000 or 5,000. The ultimate test of teaching is to handle the most profound material in the simplest language. To appreciate Christ as a teacher, get out your red-letter New Testament and read only the red-letter sections of the Gospels. Or if you are in too big a hurry for this, read the Sermon on the Mount in Matthew 5–7.

A teacher who is a genius normally has some superb students. The finest student that Christ had was John,

---

[2] Luke 9:54.   [3] Matt. 9:9–13; Mark 2:1, 13, 14.
[4] John 12:6; 13:29.

whose Gospel is read by more people than any other book in the whole Bible—and that means, of course, more than any other book in the world. This is the Gospel that a child understands and loves. This same Gospel is also loved by the most profound scholar, who frankly admits that he never plumbs its depths but is ever challenged to restudy this greatest masterpiece of world scholarship. Another pupil was Matthew the tax collector who wrote a Gospel as he saw it. He was busy balancing both sides of the ledger. It is Matthew who concentrated upon demonstrating that Christ fulfilled "the plans and specifications" of the Messiah of the Old Testament. It is he who emphasizes the essential nature of a common Bible—two Testaments, but one theme.

Matthew summarized the early Galilean ministry of Christ in these words: "And he went about all Galilee, teaching in their synagogues and preaching the gospel of the kingdom and healing every disease and every infirmity among the people. So his fame spread throughout all Syria, and they brought him all the sick, those afflicted with various diseases and pains, demoniacs, epileptics, and paralytics, and he healed them. And great crowds followed him from Galilee and the Decapolis and Jerusalem and Judea and from beyond the Jordan."[5] Mark adds that they also came from Idumea and Tyre and Sidon.[6] Thus Christ attracted men from all areas of Palestine, both east and west of the Jordan river and from the Sinai desert as far north as Beirut and Damascus.

---

[5] Matt. 4:23–25.   [6] Mark 3:8.

VIII

The Sermon on the Mount

IN ORDER TO HELP the layman who reads this book, we will follow the general pattern of the Gospel of Matthew for the ministry of Christ rather than using a harmony of the Gospels, as is the general practice of scholars. We shall add data from the other Gospels when we are dealing with related themes in Matthew. Of course, in the small compass of this book we can deal with only a few of the major themes of the Gospel story.

The Sermon on the Mount illustrates what was said in Chapter V concerning the early manhood of Christ. Here is a happy blending of many of the techniques Christ used in all of his teachings. Like the book of Psalms, the Sermon opens with the theme of happiness; "blessed" is simply happiness raised to the nth degree. But no psalmist or prophet could write this sermon, for here is *heaven's* evaluation of joy. This sermon is infinitely more than the finest social gospel that we talk about today.

Following the beatitudes, Christ fills his message with picture windows illustrating the beatitudes in terms of everyday life. Let us look at a few of these picture windows.

"You are the salt of the earth; but if salt has lost its taste, how shall its saltness be restored? It is no longer good for anything except to be thrown out and trodden under foot by men."[1]

Salt was one of the essentials of life and so important that it was an object of taxation. Turkey was still using this tax in the Near East before World War I. Our word "salary" comes from the money given the Roman soldier for his salt ration. Salt from the marshes along the Mediterranean and the Dead Sea[2] was impure and lost its flavor when exposed to the earth as in storage. Nevertheless, its chemical composition was such that it would destroy vegetation if thrown into a field, so the only safe place to dispose of it was in the street of a town or village. The Christian is the true salt of the earth.

"You are the light of the world. A city set on a hill cannot be hid."[3]

This and the next parable illustrate the subject of visibility. The city on a hill can best be explained by the photograph on page 66. Jesus may have been referring to the Hellenistic city of Hippos across the lake. But he was also talking about the normal city of Old Testament and intertestament times. All such cities were located on hilltops or on the isolated spur of a hill, because these were ideal defensive positions.[4] Jerusalem, for example, although on the spur of a hill, was virtually impregnable, except from the north where there was only a shallow valley. David captured the city not by assault but by sending a commando unit up through the water system of the city. Shechem was one of the few Old Testament cities built in a valley where there was a mountain just behind it.

Then Christ used the illustration of a lamp, saying in

---

[1] Matt. 5:13.   [2] Ezek. 47:10–11.   [3] Matt. 5:14.

[4] In Palestine the word *tell* on a map refers to a walled city and is usually from Old Testament times. *Khirbeh* refers to one of the towns or cities of the Roman period which are normally on the plain or at the base of a hill and usually unfortified.

substance, "You do not light a lamp and then put a bushel basket over it." The lamp was invented to give light, therefore "let your light so shine before men, that they may see your good works and give glory to your Father who is in heaven."[5]

Jesus also used the lamp in the parable of the wise and foolish virgins.[6] These were very small lamps (less than three inches long), and when carried out of doors, as in this story, they were probably placed on pottery saucers to collect the oil that would be spilled as the girls walked. What oil remained in the lamps would quickly burn away, and the lamps would have to be refilled. Therefore, any thoughtful girl going to a wedding always took along a little jar of olive oil to replenish her lamp. (This parable shows that there were careless teen-agers in those days too.) These little lamps were molded by native Palestinian potters and were probably made in the same town where they were used.

The whole problem of ethics in the ancient world is a fascinating one. As the archaeologist reads the old legal codes, he sees a slow but gradual improvement in ethics. This was not a gradual evolutionary improvement since there were some striking peaks and some sickening depressions in this graph of ethical advance. But the mean average is a gradual improvement in idealism. Actual practice, of course, lagged behind the ideal in all generations.

With the coming of Christ, ethics suddenly becomes something completely different, something uniquely new. Now we have Christ himself and his own standards as par! "You, therefore, must be perfect, as your heavenly Father is perfect."[7] Paul caught the essence of the new ethical demand when he said, "Be imitators of me, as I am of Christ."[8] The Pharisees and the Essenes were also deeply interested in ethics, but to contrast their teaching with Christ, nothing will be as helpful as to read the Mishnah

---

[5] Matt. 5:16. [6] Matt. 25:1–13. [7] Matt. 5:48. [8] I Cor. 11:1.

(primarily a Pharisee work) and the rules of the Essene community.

Matthew 5:43 is of special significance in contrasting the ethic of the Essenes with that of Christ. "You have heard that it was said, 'You shall love your neighbor and hate your enemy.' " Neither the Old Testament nor any extant early rabbinic writings teach "hate your enemy." On the other hand, however, it was the duty of the Essenes to hate everyone whom God had rejected. They were also to hate the sons of darkness. And the hatred of which the Essenes spoke was eternal hatred.

In Matthew 6:2–4 Jesus discussed almsgiving. This was a major feature of Jewish theology in the intertestament period. It was heavily stressed and became virtually a doctrine of "justification by works." Tobit, the earliest of the Apocryphal books, dating back to Persian times, emphasizes almsgiving over and over. Even if you are poor you must give alms.[9] "Alms delivers from death, and it shall purge away all sin."[10] Ecclesiasticus 3:30 also stresses that "alms giving will make atonement for sin."

In commenting upon the way in which these Jewish leaders gave their alms, Christ refers to them as hypocrites. To the archaeologist this is a most interesting word, as it is one of the few uniquely Greek terms that Christ used. It comes from the Greek theatre which had been introduced to Palestine in the intertestament period. Sepphoris had its Greek theatre during the boyhood of Jesus, as did Jerusalem and all the cities which Herod the Great built. The word *hypocrite* means an actor on the stage, i.e., a man who pretends to be something which he is not. Christ used the word fifteen different times in his sermons. His most frequent use of it was during Passion Week, when he employed it eight times.

When Christ dealt with the theme of judgment, he illustrated it from his carpenter shop.[11] Literally translated Matthew 7:3 reads, "Why do you see the splinter that is in

---

[9] Tobit 4:8. [10] Tobit 12:9. [11] Matt. 7:1–5.

This is the northern shore of the Sea of Galilee with Capernaum toward right center. The road to Nazareth went through the ridge gap toward left center.

Fishing in the Sea of Galilee.

*"City set on a hill"
—a typical
Palestinian tell.*

Below: *This ancient lava flow east of Galilee makes fertile soil for wheat. Old volcanoes stand on the horizon.* Bottom: *A colonnaded street passes in front of the Roman theatre in Amman which was cut out of the solid rock of the mountain.*

your brother's eye but do not see the roof beam in your own eye?" These Semitic hyperboles were one of the characteristics of Christ's teaching method. Another well-known example is the following: "It is easier for a camel to go through the eye of a needle than for a rich man to enter the kingdom of God."[12]

The city gate of Matthew 7:13 is another carpenter's term. It was made of heavy timber studded over with heavy iron sheeting so that neither fire nor battering ram could destroy it quickly. The "wide gate" was the main gate of the city, wide enough for chariots to enter. The "narrow gate" was the sortie gate in a section of the city wall where a small detachment of soldiers could leave the city suddenly and fall upon the beseigers and then quickly retreat through this same sortie gate to the safety of the city.

In Matthew 7:17 it is again the woodsman who contrasts the sound tree with the decaying one. The latter, although a fruit tree, had no future except as firewood. The former, however, could continue as a fruit tree or be cut up into useful lumber. The best of such trees were the olive and the carob, both of which would take an excellent finish. The carob tree produced the long beans which are called husks in the parable of the prodigal son.

The Sermon on the Mount closes with the picture of two houses caught in a cloudburst. This parable of foundations, one built on the rock and one built on the ground, interests the archaeologist, for foundations are often all that is left of a building for him to study. The parable comes in two versions—one in Matthew 7:24–27 and the other in Luke 6:47–49. Both these houses were built in the valley, and the major factor in each case is a flash flood following a cloudburst. These cloudbursts are so common that the Hebrew language even uses "cloudburst" as a verb.

In Luke's version, one builder goes down deep through

---

[12] Matt. 19:24.

surface soil until he hits bedrock and lays his foundation. The other house was built directly on the ground without any real foundation; therefore, when the flash flood hit, that house immediately fell. Matthew gives an abridged edition of the building of each house, but adds that the poor house was built on sandy soil. The damage of a usual storm is to the roof which was covered with a compact marly clay, or to the marly clay plaster used to surface the irregular fieldstone wall. But the storm of this parable is a cloudburst with its resulting flash flood. Life is like this latter storm with its deadly devastation.

The genius of Jesus as a teacher is seen at the conclusion of the Sermon on the Mount. "And when Jesus finished these sayings, the crowds were astonished at his teaching, for he taught them as one who had authority, and not as their scribes."[13]

---

[13] Matt. 7:28–29.

IX

Christ's Continuing Ministry

AFTER GIVING the Sermon on the Mount, Christ returned to Capernaum. As he neared the city he was urged to heal a servant of the centurion who was in charge of the military detachment there.[1] This officer was such a zealous convert to Judaism that he had built the synagogue at Capernaum at his own expense. And this was the synagogue in which Christ regularly worshiped. But the centurion's understanding of the Old Testament was still more significant than this magnificent charity, for he recognized *obedience* as the key word in the godly life. The centurion answered Christ, " 'Lord, I am not worthy to have you come under my roof; but only say the word, and my servant will be healed. For I am a man under authority, with soldiers under me; and I say to one, "Go," and he goes, and to another, "Come," and he comes, and to my slave, "Do this," and he does it.' When Jesus heard him, he marveled, and said to those who followed him, 'Truly I say to you, not even in Israel have I found such faith.' "[2]

Most Bible students have seen pictures of the partially

---

[1] Matt. 8:5–13.   [2] Matt. 8:8–10.

restored synagogue at Capernaum, but this is an early third century edifice and not the one in which Christ worshiped. There is some evidence, however, that the present synagogue rests upon the foundations of the synagogue of Christ's day. Up to the present, no synagogue of New Testament times has been excavated in Palestine. All of these seem to have been destroyed, either in the first Jewish revolt against Rome that ended in the destruction of Jerusalem in A.D. 70, or in the second revolt in A.D. 135, when Judaism was almost annihilated in Palestine.

If the centurion's synagogue was built of limestone, as was the one now seen on the site, then it would have stood out brilliantly in contrast to the whole city of Capernaum. The houses of that city were built of basalt, which is about the deadest black stone that can be used for building purposes. Capernaum was built on a great black lava flow. Across the Sea of Galilee is the same lava flow with dead volcanoes lined along the eastern horizon. But if the city was colorless and drab, its surroundings were in brilliant kodachrome. The deep blue Sea of Galilee lies 600 feet below sea level, and the mountains on either side are reflecting basins, making the lake area a first-rate hothouse. The rich soil from an earlier lakebed plus the decaying lava and the soil deposits of the winter rains produced a very luxuriant vegetation. Far in the distance to the north Mt. Hermon, snow-covered during much of the year, was visible from many places along the lake.

Returning to Christ's healing ministry at Capernaum, there is a highly significant episode when a paralytic is brought to Jesus by his friends. Christ said to him, " 'Take heart, my son; your sins are forgiven.' And behold, some of the scribes said to themselves, 'This man is blaspheming.' But Jesus, knowing their thoughts, said, 'Why do you think evil in your hearts? For which is easier, to say, 'Your sins are forgiven,' or to say, 'Rise and walk'? But that you may know that the Son of man has authority on earth to forgive sins'—he then said to the paralytic—'Rise, take up your bed and go home.' . . . When the crowds saw it, they were afraid, and they glorified God, who had given such authority to men."[3]

It is in the presence of such an episode as this that the Christian archaeologist stands amazed: "The Son of man has authority on earth to forgive sins." Instantly Christ is unique. Archaeology knows no match to the authority and finality of this remark in all of ancient history. Church history, however, has vindicated this unique truth that Christ does forgive sins and that Christ is the only solution to death!

Two other healings are of special interest to us around Capernaum. One was the case of Peter's mother-in-law. Luke the physician describes it as follows: "Simon's mother-in-law was ill with a high fever, and they besought him for her. And he stood over her and rebuked the fever, and it left her; and immediately she arose and served them."[4] Numerous scholars identify the fever with malaria, which is still common in the swampy sections of Palestine. The excavators at Megiddo and Beth-shan were handicapped by malaria and had to arrange digging dates to avoid this scourge.

Upon returning to work one morning at New Testament Jericho, we found that the irrigation ditch above the excavation had overflowed during the night, and its excess water had filled the great reflecting basin built by Herod the Great before Christ was born. We naturally allowed the water to stay there so we could check on the workmanship of Herod's builders. The plaster lining of the reflecting basin proved to be watertight over 1900 years after it was applied! Several days later, however, the Arabs reminded us that this was a malaria district and the water must go lest the malarial mosquitos breed in it.

Another miracle of healing was the occasion when Christ actually touched a leper in the healing of that malady.[5] The mere touching of the leper was a violation of Jewish law; therefore, this act of mercy would have sent a

---

[3] Matt. 9:2–8.   [4] Luke 4:38–39.   [5] Luke 5:13.

71

shudder through all the witnesses of this healing. At that time it was not known that leprosy was the least contagious of all such tropical diseases. Today missionaries spend a lifetime working in the leper colonies and only rarely contract the disease.

The tenth chapter of Matthew lists the twelve disciples whom Christ later empowered as apostles, that is, envoys or delegates appointed by him and responsible to him alone. Fairly early in his ministry Christ was already sending out his students to do what he himself had been doing.[6] But he also warned them of the reception they would receive later when he as the resurrected Christ would send them out for the evangelization of the whole world. One wonders what these men thought when he gave them these orders.[7] After the Transfiguration, Christ sent out "the seventy" upon a similar task. Thus Christ put the *laity* to doing the *same work* as the apostles![8]

Later Christ condemned Chorazin and Beth-saida, neighboring towns to Capernaum, saying that it would be more tolerable for Tyre and Sidon in the judgment than for these cities that had rejected his message.[9] (Remember that people from Tyre and Sidon were among those who had come to hear Christ.) The historical reference is to the days when Jezebel, daughter of the king of Tyre, tried to convert the kingdom of Israel from Jehovah-worship to Baal-worship—an action which pitted her against Elijah. Her daughter Athaliah actually usurped the Davidic throne in Jerusalem where for a brief time she established Baal-worship in Solomon's Temple itself! Later heretical Judean monarchs added Moloch worship, the worst of all the Baal cults, for it demanded child sacrifice! Whole centers of infant sacrifices to Moloch have been found around Carthage, a colony of Tyre. Contrast Christ's attitude toward little children.

The condemnation of unrepentant Capernaum was still stronger "And you, Capernaum, will you be exalted to

---

[6] Matt. 10:5ff.   [7] Matt. 10:16ff.   [8] Luke 10:1–20.   [9] Matt. 11:20–22.

heaven? You shall be brought down to Hades. For if the mighty works done in you had been done in Sodom, it would have remained until this day. But I tell you that it shall be more tolerable on the day of judgment for the land of Sodom than for you."[10] This contrast takes us back to Abraham himself and his great intercessory prayer for Sodom. But Sodom had already committed the unpardonable sin and had to be punished. The same was now true of Capernaum. Both had to go. The wages of sin is death; this applies not only to individuals but to cities and nations as well. How tragic was Capernaum's doom. Men without number came here for bodily healing and found a perfect healing of the flesh. But the same city rejected the healing of its soul. Capernaum had seen God face to face, but it had rejected him!

After his remarks on these cities where his ministry was concentrated, Christ begins his comments about babes and children. "I thank thee, Father, Lord of heaven and earth, that thou hast hidden these things from the wise and understanding and revealed them to babes."[11] In Christ's attitude toward little children the archaeologist again sees something new and unique in theological thinking. Christ is putting the emphasis on *trust and obedience*—the key virtues of a child reared in a Jewish home of his day. These were also the characteristics of Christ himself in his relationship to his heavenly Father through every day of his earthly life.

Christ also emphasized the traits of trust and obedience after his transfiguration. "At that time the disciples came to Jesus, saying, 'Who is the greatest in the kingdom of heaven?' And calling to him a child, he put him in the midst of them, and said, 'Truly, I say to you, unless you turn and become like children, you will never enter the kingdom of heaven. Whoever humbles himself like this child, he is the greatest in the kingdom of heaven.' "[12]

He then adds, "Whoever causes one of these little ones

---

[10] Matt. 11:23-24.   [11] Matt. 11:25.   [12] Matt. 18:1-4.

73

who believes in me to sin, it would be better for him to have a great millstone fashioned round his neck and to be drowned in the depth of the sea."[13]

At Capernaum today the visitors can see the cone-shaped base of a large stone upon which turned the doughnut-shaped unit which ground the flour. This millstone may have been used by the military detachment at Capernaum. Khirbet Qumran shows a complete mill with both upper and lower units. The upper stone is the one to which Christ refers, and if twenty-five people were tied to one of these millstones, they would probably all drown in the depth of the sea so heavy is that stone. (Incidentally Christ was no pacifist where children were concerned!)

Mark records (in 10:16) that Christ took little children "in his arms and blessed them, laying his hands upon them." Remember that such a "blessing" is given only by God, and in this episode Christ is expressing his deity.

Later Christ withdrew to the district of Tyre and Sidon and here met one of the most unique persons in all his ministry—a Syrophoenician Greek woman praying for her little girl. "And he said to her, 'Let the children first be fed, for it is not right to take the children's bread and throw it to the dogs.' But she answered him, 'Yes, Lord; yet even the dogs under the table eat the children's crumbs.' "[14]

The story needs only one comment for modern readers. Most of us like dogs for pets, and as a nation we spend more money on dogs than on foreign missions. But in the Near East, even the pet dog, which is the kind of dog Jesus is referring to here, was considered an outcast and a scavenger by adults. The children, of course, who played with these dogs, gave them a much higher rating. In religious terminology the word was reserved for a degenerate.[15] This woman is one of the few characters in the Gospels who rose to the full height of Christ's challenge! Like the Roman centurion, she was not Jewish by birth.

The climax of Christ's teaching on children is at the

---

[13] Matt. 18:6.   [14] Mark 7:27–28.   [15] Deut. 23:18.

This child is wearing modern Arab dress similar to that which was worn in Bible times. Jesus welcomed children and warned that anyone who led a child astray deserved to be drowned with a millstone hung around his neck. He referred to a stone like this one (below) from Pompeii which was turned by either a man or a donkey.

Below: *Ruins of the third-century synagogue at Capernaum.*

Galilee to the west of Caesarea Philippi.

Caesarea Philippi was in the foothills of Mount Hermon which is snow covered most of the year. Below: Syrophoenician country. A shepherd waters his goats by the Litany River.

Lord's Supper when he calls his disciples "little children." Here Christ identifies himself with the disciples in the strongest descriptive term he could use, for like a parent he is now ready to lay down his life for the children. But at the same time these disciples for whom he is laying down his life are often, after all, only little children in the things of the Spirit, even after their three years' work with Christ. They really did not know the true significance of what he was teaching them until after the gift of the Holy Spirit at Pentecost.

X

God Comes to Caesarea Philippi

CAESAREA Philippi is an archaeologist's paradise because of its long history and its ultimate significance. The setting of the city is near an exquisitely beautiful, copious spring which is one of the four sources of the Jordan River. George Adam Smith in his *Historical Geography of the Holy Land* gives the following description:

You pass a well-watered meadow, covered by trees, and then a broad terrace, with oaks, like an English park, till you come to the edge of a deep gorge, through which there roars a headlong stream, half stifled by bush. An old Roman bridge takes you over, and then through a tangle of trees, brushwood and fern you break into sight of a high cliff of limestone, reddened by the water that oozes over its face from the iron soil above. In the cliff is a cavern. Part of the upper rock has fallen, and from the debris of boulders and shingle below there bursts and bubbles along a line of thirty feet a full-born river. The place is a very sanctuary of waters, and from time immemorial men have drawn near it to worship. As you stand within the charm of it—and this is a charm not uncommon in the Lebanons—you understand why the early Semites adored the Baalim of the subterranean waters even

78

before they raised their gods to heaven, and thanked them for the rain.[1]

In early Palestinian history this great cave with a full-born stream emerging from it and watering a fertile plain was a perfect sanctuary for the Canaanite fertility god Baal! When the Greeks came in under Alexander the Great, they adopted this beautiful natural sanctuary as their own and dedicated it to their god Pan, who was a sort of second cousin to Baal. Later Herod the Great rebuilt an older city near this sanctuary and named it Caesarea in honor of his patron Augustus Caesar. But close by the sacred cave, as at Samaria, he built a temple, and here too he dedicated it to the worship of the divine Augustus!

It is near this age-old sanctuary of many faiths that Christ asked his disciples, "Who do men say that I am?" "Simon Peter replied, 'You are the Christ, the Son of the living God.' And Jesus answered him, 'Blessed are you, Simon Bar-Jona! For flesh and blood has not revealed this to you, but my Father who is in heaven.' "[2] Jesus' response to Peter is extremely significant, for here, where human reason had deified both nature and man, Jesus is now acknowledged as the Christ, the Son of the living God by revelation and revelation alone. Human nature had not only falsely deified nature and man, but it had failed even to recognize God when He talked to them face to face, in the person of Jesus the Christ.

After the Transfiguration, Christ must set his feet toward Jerusalem and death! But when he came down from the mountain, there was an epileptic boy that his disciples had not been able to help, so they called on Jesus. He was distressed about this and a little impatient and said, "How long am I to bear with you?"[3] Nevertheless, he stopped and healed the boy. *Do you disciples not realize that infinitely beyond the problems of life are the* problems of death, *and it is that problem toward which I am now*

---

[1] London: Hodder and Stoughton, 1896, pp. 473–474.
[2] Matt. 16:15–17.   [3] Matt. 17:17.

setting my feet? For Christ himself, their problem of life
—the problem of miraculous healing—was as nothing in
his ministry compared to the imminent problem of his own
death. Not the problem of raising people from the dead as
he did with the daughter of Jairus, the widow's son at Nain,
and Lazarus. No, his problem is the ultimate problem of
problems—sin and death and hell—the problem of the
cross. It is not until death itself is solved that one can
know what LIFE is.

While we are here with the King of kings at the Transfiguration story, let us look at two of his parables on the
Kingdom which are especially significant to the archaeologist. "The Kingdom of heaven is like treasure hidden in a
field, which a man found and covered up; then in his joy he
goes and sells all that he has and buys that field."[4] This is
a picture of every Arab farmer. The heavy flooding winter
rains sometimes wash away the soil above a tomb.
Instantly the farmer who owns the land opens the tomb
expecting to find it full of gold. If a neighbor happens to
see this exposed tomb before the owner of the land does,
the neighbor will cover up the tomb with soil and try at
once to buy the farm even at an exorbitant mortgage.

I shall never forget a day when we were excavating at
Kiriath-sepher. Suddenly an Arab workman disappeared
from sight with a shriek as the ground he was working on
gave way beneath him. In a moment he recovered himself
and asked for a flashlight. He was not interested as to
whether or not he had injured himself in the fall. The one
thing he thought of was *buried treasure!* He was gone for
a long time. When he finally came back to the opening, he
said, "Oh, they were poor people just like us." The cave
into which he had fallen had been used by the Israelites of
the time of Jeremiah as a storage area for provisioning
their army. There was no gold there.

The next verses in Christ's sermon read, "Again, the
kingdom of heaven is like a merchant in search of fine

---

[4] Matt. 13:44.

pearls, who, on finding one pearl of great value, went and sold all that he had and bought it."[5] Here again one finds something which is priceless and for which everything must be mortgaged.

Most of us modern readers of Scripture fail to appreciate the use of precious stones and pearls in antiquity. They were not only valuable then as now for adornment, but they were also the ideal way to carry wealth. Gold is heavy. Its weight gives it away to alert robbers. But pearls and precious stones can be wrapped up in a tiny package and concealed anywhere on the person. It was the equivalent of carrying all their wealth in thousand dollar bills—or a king's ransom in twenty thousands. Even today you can see, as we have, the economics of this parable in some of the little jewelry stores in Jerusalem where men deal only in the best of gems and pearls.

These two short parables tell us that the Kingdom of heaven is priceless. Any normal man should recognize its value and seek to obtain it at all costs.

A king's banquet hall is a good place to study Christ's parable of those seeking the chief seats.[6] This parable was beautifully demonstrated to us one day at Beer-sheba shortly after World War I. There had been a very bad locust plague in the Negeb and Sinai areas, and the British had enlisted the aid of the Bedouin tribes to help in combating the plague. The British not only paid them for the work, but following the normal Arab pattern of giving a feast at the close of work, a special holiday was arranged for them. This included sports, camel racing, American movies, and a banquet.

The long black goat hair tents of the Bedouin sheiks were lined up for the ceremony. We watched Arab dignitaries seeking honored places at these tents. Some of these visitors were received with dignity; others were quickly thrown out, each of the latter tumbling over the

---

[5] Matt. 13:45, 46.   [6] Luke 14:7–11.

long Turkish sword worn at his belt as a sign of prestige. These discards then tried to enter the next tent of lower rank. Some would be received here, others were again thrown out. Each man tried until he finally found his own rank, low as it might be.

In the beginning of this chapter we were at Caesarea Philippi in the northern section of the Tetrarchy of Philip. Let us close the chapter on the border of this territory just north of the Decapolis. Laymen are often surprised to see Christ involved with hogs; but note that the major episode in which they are involved[7] is in Transjordan, most of which was Greek. Much of the area was called the Decapolis, a Greek term for an alliance of ten city-states. In the period after the death of Alexander the Great, the Near East went Greek, and in many ways the change was as great as the Westernization of modern Japan. In the Decapolis as in Japan, it was not an influx of foreigners, but primarily a change of culture by the original inhabitants.

In the intertestament period Rabbath-Ammon, the capital of the Ammonites, was renamed Philadelphia by Ptolemy Philadelphus, king of Egypt, and one of the most cultured Greeks of his time. Jerash is today the best preserved city of the Decapolis. It is often called the Pompeii of Palestine. The ruins of this Greek city are largely from after Christ's time, but the architectural changes were in minor features only. So the best way to get an idea of what Jerusalem looked like in Christ's time is to visit Jerash today.

The conclusion of the story of the Gadarene demoniac that Christ healed is as tragic and as modern as today. Hogs are still more important than the mentally ill. At least that is the attitude of the U.S. government which has enabled us to lead the world in hog culture, but not in research for the mentally distressed.

---

[7] Matt. 8:28–34.

Left:
*Main street
of Jerash.*

Below: *Civic center
of Jerash
from one of the
two theatres
of that city.*

XI

Matthew and Money

THE ANCIENT Israelites insisted on following three false gods: (1) Baalism, more commonly called idolatry; (2) Money, and (3) Philosophy. The first Israelite heresy was largely gone by New Testament times, although the Gentiles of the world were still enthusiastic devotees at their idol shrines—witness the riot at Ephesus.

The money heresy came to Israel with the introduction of the manufacturing age about the time of Isaiah, in the eighth century B.C. And the nation's new economic leaders were also soon dominant in the religious field as well. Although the prophets preached against the new Mammon, as they did the older Baal, they were unsuccessful. The Mosaic code had been an ideal law book for an agricultural nation; but no prophet arose who was able to give Israel a code of ethics for use in the manufacturing age.

After the destruction of Jerusalem in 587 B.C. two new economic features entered Israel's economic life. The first was banking, which her people learned as exiles in the Babylonian captivity. This profession was later to make the Jews a strong economic block in the eastern half of the Roman empire. The second economic change was Persia's unique theory of government which (1) fostered a common world trade from India to the Balkans; (2) accepted Aramaic rather than Persian as the business language of its empire, and (3) gave to all tributary lands one common international coinage. Also, during the intertestament period Alexander's methods of sharing the spoils of war with his soldiers did more to put money in circulation among the common people than anything up to his time.

In the days of Christ money was still the same false god of the Jews that it had been in the days of the early prophets. The remarks which Christ makes relative to money as recorded in Matthew's Gospel[1] demonstrate that money was one of Christ's greatest competitors during his ministry. Christ's thesis on money is succinctly stated in one verse: "No one can serve two masters; for either he will hate the one and love the other, or he will be devoted to the one and despise the other. You cannot serve God and mammon."[2]

The Sermon on the Mount begins, "Blessed are the poor in spirit."[3] Luke phrases it, "Blessed are you poor."[4] The student of Hebrew has no trouble here, as the Hebrew concept of "poor" is both economic and spiritual; thus both Matthew and Luke are correct. The Sermon on the Mount is for "the poor." This can be seen later in the Sermon—Christ taught his disciples to pray "Give us this day our 'day by day' bread" (a rather literal translation). The poor earned only enough in one day for one day's food.

Jesus Christ came with good news for "the poor." His mission was to them. The Messianic pattern which he must fulfill was set for him in Isaiah 55:1:

> "Ho, every one who thirsts,
>   come to the waters;
> and he who has no money,
>   come, buy and eat!
> Come, buy wine and milk
>   without money and without price."

Jesus confirmed both this good news and his Messiahship to the deputation which John the Baptist sent to him. The

---

[1] Luke also contributes to the money thesis.   [2] Matt. 6:24.
[3] Matt. 5:3.   [4] Luke 6:20.

climax of his reply was ". . . and the poor have good news preached to them."[5]

It is blessed to be poor, then, because one can "buy" good things without money. And perhaps having money would incline one to disregard this kind of good news.

Christ's concern over the false god of Mammon is further seen in his words, "Do not lay up for yourselves treasures on earth, where moth and rust consume and where thieves break in and steal, but lay up for yourselves treasures in heaven, where neither moth nor rust consumes and where thieves do not break in and steal. *For where your treasure is, there will your heart be also*" (italics mine).[6] This is why Christ said no one can serve two masters. You have to chose between treasure in heaven and treasure on earth, between God and money.

After his Transfiguration, Jesus said to his disciples, "What will it profit a man, if he gains the whole world and forfeits his life? . . . For the Son of man is to come with his angels in the glory of his Father, and then he will repay every man for what he has done."[7] Christ spoke as a man of experience on the subject of wealth and temptation to gain all at a huge cost. He gave up heaven to die for a lost world! And he had faced and rejected this temptation when Satan offered the world to him immediately following his baptism.

The unconscious hold that wealth can lay on a good moral man is illustrated in the episode of the rich young ruler.[8] He insisted to Christ that he had kept all the Ten Commandments. Christ, the ideal teacher, began by examining the young man on his observance of the first commandment. He demonstrated that this young ruler had flunked the first commandment, because gold, not God, was the essential worship pattern of his life. The young man "went away sorrowful; for he had great possessions."

Jesus then turned to his disciples and said, "Truly, I say to you, it will be hard for a rich man to enter the kingdom

---

[5] Matt. 11:5. [6] Matt. 6:19–21. [7] Matt. 16:26–27. [8] Matt. 19:16–30.

of heaven. Again I tell you, it is easier for a camel to go through the eye of a needle than for a rich man to enter the kingdom of God." When the disciples asked, "Who then can be saved?" Jesus replied that what is impossible with men is possible with God. Then he told them the parable of the laborers in the vineyard.[9]

Although this parable was spoken by Christ over 1900 years ago, we have seen similar day laborers at sunrise or even earlier waiting in the marketplace for someone to hire them for that day. Those not employed waited through the long day in hope of getting work for at least a few hours. Meanwhile some of those who had been employed earlier found that their work lasted for only a few hours, and so they returned to seek more employment.

The crux of the parable comes at evening when the owner of the vineyard pays each workman a denarius (a normal day's wage) regardless of whether he had worked all day or as little as one hour. Human nature is the same in all ages, and those who had worked from sunrise to sunset naturally growled about what they thought was the injustice of the owner who had paid them no more than the latecomers.

But the godly owner of the vineyard knew that the laborer's family would eat their one meal of the day only if the laborer was employed that day. If the workman went unemployed, his family went hungry that day, or were fed only at the mercy of their neighbors. So the gracious owner of the vineyard gave each man enough money to feed his own family that evening. Even today in certain fishing ports in Arabia the catch is divided not according to the number of men who work in the boat but according to the size of their families.

At another time Jesus intensified this aspect of the employer's mercy (in Luke 17:7–10). He had been talking about a servant's or employee's responsibility, and concluded, "When you have done all that is commanded you,

---

[9] Matt. 20:1–16.

say, 'We are unworthy servants; we have only done what was our duty.' "

Later Matthew follows Christ around during Passion Week and watches Christ clean out the godless commercialism of the Temple which the religious leaders of the Jews were carrying on as a private monopoly.[10] All their commercialism was contrary to the Mosaic law, although they insisted that they were in complete subjection to that code. Here in the Temple itself the theme is again, "You cannot serve God and Mammon." And since Christ had already cleansed the Temple at the very beginning of his ministry, this second sin was distinctly unpardonable. It amounted to virtually an adoration of what we would call today the Almighty Dollar!

Later in the week the Jewish leaders tried to entrap Christ by asking, "Is it lawful to pay taxes to Caesar, or not?"[11] He evaded their dilemma by simply saying, "Render therefore to Caesar the things that are Caesar's, and to God the things that are God's."[12] There is humor in this episode, in that when Christ asked them for a coin, they had one ready to give him—a *Roman* denarius, the coin most commonly used for paying tribute to Caesar! All the wealth of the Jewish clergy was in *Roman* money. Roman money was the only legal tender in which they could amass their fortunes; and it was only Roman money which could purchase their luxuries. Every one of these men would have been a pauper without Roman money. Luke puts his finger on the heart of the problem when he says of the Pharisees that they were "lovers of money."[13]

At the end of Passion week Judas betrayed Christ for thirty pieces of silver—God himself was traded for cold cash! Tragically Christ is still traded for cold cash in our own day.

What then was Christ's attitude toward wealth? It was identical with that taught in the Old Testament.

---

[10] Matt. 21:12–13.   [11] Matt. 22:17.   [12] Matt. 22:21.   [13] Luke 16:14.

Condensed into a single word, Christ's attitude toward money was *stewardship*.

Since this chapter deals with money, let us look at some of the coins mentioned in the Gospels. The denarius was the most common silver coin used in the Roman Empire. It was minted under the emperor's directions and had an official weight of 3.8 grams. This coin was used as the legal tender for paying tribute to Rome, and that city in turn paid her soldiers with this coin. In Palestine it was the wage paid a day laborer who worked from sunrise to sunset. It is mentioned more often than any other coin in the Gospels.

The drachma had been the official coin of the Greeks before Rome came to power, and it was still in use in New Testament times, but its silver content was doubtless reduced to the equivalent of that of the denarius. A sheep could be purchased for a drachma and a pair of oxen for ten drachma. Keep these figures in mind as you read the parable of the lost coin which was a drachma.[14] The woman in this parable lost a coin of real value.

When the archeologist is tearing down house walls he occasionally finds coins hidden in between the stones of these walls. Such crannies in the walls were the safety deposit vaults of those in the lower income brackets. The archeologist visualizes this woman not only sweeping the house but also using a lamp as she searched the crannies in the wall and tried to remember just where she had hidden that drachma.

Judas betrayed Christ for thirty pieces of silver (the literal translation is thirty silvers).[15] This coin is thought to be either the shekel of Tyre or the tetradrachma of Antioch. The market value in this transaction according to the Mosaic law was the equivalent of the money paid for the death of a slave gored by a neighbor's ox.[16] Another

---

[14] Luke 15:8-10.   [15] Zech. 11:12.   [16] Exod. 21:32.

evaluation of the thirty silvers rated Christ "the good shepherd" as worth 120 sheep.

The "widow's mite" of the King James Bible was a tiny copper coin about the size of the nail on your little finger.[17] This was the smallest coin in use, and it took almost 150 of these to equal the value of one silver denarius.

The archaeologist is also interested in the mintage story of each coin he finds. Our seminary has a coin found in Palestine which had been minted in Gaul (modern France). What a history this coin must have had en route to Palestine! The seminary also has a coin minted by Pontius Pilate of the year A.D. 30, which is the date many scholars give for the crucifixion of Christ.

At Bethel we dug up a "silver" coin from the period of the late Roman Empire, but the metal was so debased with cheap alloy that the silver had a brass tint. Today our nation is following a related depreciation by putting copper centers in our "silver" coins.

---

[17] Luke 21:2; Mark 12:42.

XII

Jewish Philosophy vs. Christ's Teaching

GREEK PHILOSOPHY did not make a strong imprint on Jewish religious teaching until about the time of the Maccabees (165 B.C.), although the center of Greek culture had moved from Athens to Alexandria c. 300 B.C. under the influence of Ptolemy Lagi, and the Old Testament translation into Greek was begun about the same time. The Sadducees were the first to take up Greek philosophy for theological purposes, but the Pharisees soon became its chief exponents.

The first five books of the Bible became the essential field of philosophic work by the Jews; and their projects were (1) a logical expansion of the Mosaic laws to fit the Jewish life of that day, (2) an attempt to work out something of a creed based on the data of these laws. Unfortunately, they did not work on the *totality* of the Old Testament, and they were especially weak in the Messianic interpretation of the Old Testament.

One point of emphasis by these Pharisee legalists was the Sabbath. To really appreciate the vast difference between the views of Jesus and the Jewish leaders, one should read the thirty-six pages of the legal rulings on Sabbath observance that appear in the Mishnah, which was second only to the Mosaic code itself. Notice how Jesus handled the Sabbath problem with the Jews. In one episode,[1] "the ruler of the synagogue, indignant because Jesus had healed on the sabbath, said to the people, 'There are six days on which work ought to be done; come on those days and be healed, and not on the sabbath day.'" To this criticism Jesus replied *ad hominem,* "You hypocrites! Does not each of you on the sabbath untie his ox or his ass from the manger, and lead it away to water it? And ought not this woman, a daughter of Abraham whom Satan bound for eighteen years, be loosed from this bond on the sabbath day?" In John 7:22–23 Christ also calls attention to the Mosaic law which permits circumcision on the Sabbath.

The Pharisees also criticized Jesus for allowing his disciples to eat "soft wheat" on the Sabbath as they passed through the grain fields.[2] Christ replied in substance: *Don't you know your Bible? David is your ideal, and yet he broke the Mosaic law when he went into the sanctuary and ate "the bread of the Presence, which it was not lawful for him to eat." Again, do you not know that in your Mosaic law the priests profane the Sabbath by working at their sacrificial duties? Yet they are blameless.* Then Christ clinched his argument by insisting that "the Son of man is lord of the sabbath"; therefore, whatever he did was correct!

In the fifth chapter of John, Christ was again rebuked for healing a man on the Sabbath. Christ reminded them that he was not only "Lord of the Sabbath" but that he was equal with God the Father—with the result that "the Jews sought all the more to kill him." Replying to their criticism of his deity he then affirmed at length the relationship between God the Father and God the Son. Then again Christ rebuked them because they refused to believe him on this point as they had already refused to accept Moses on Sabbath observance. Their logic was helpless in the

---

[1] Luke 13:10–17.   [2] Matt. 12:1–8.

Above: *The courtyard of the Jerusalem Temple extended across all the area of this photo. The Muslim "Dome of the Rock" in the center is on the site of the Temple. The mosque at the extreme right was a Crusader church. It is in the area which Herod the Great added to the courtyard of Solomon's Temple.*

Right: *The Pool of Bethzatha (Bethesda) is below these excavations. You can see the difference in ground levels between Christ's day and the present.*

Below: *A watchtower in a vineyard.*

presence of Christ's doctrine of the Sabbath and his doctrine of the Trinity. Here he demonstrated that *revelation is the only sufficient source of knowledge about God.*

When we are talking about the Sabbath day, we should remember that the creation story in Genesis did not have its climax in the creation of man but in the doctrine of the Sabbath. After the resurrection, Christ was to have still more to say about the Sabbath.[3]

Another characteristic of these Jewish philosophers was to demand of Christ a sign or miracle whenever his argument outwitted them in logic or whenever he did anything which was not included under "the tradition of the elders." This asking for a sign was used not only by the enemies of Christ but also by his disciples. Everyone was insisting that Jesus as the Messiah must work super-miracles—something beyond the miracles of Moses and Elijah.

There is often real humor in the insistence. Sometimes the people would say, "Now give us a sign," immediately after Christ had worked a miracle. For example, Christ had just fed the five thousand, yet when he requested their allegiance they still asked him for a sign![4] They did the same after the feeding of the four thousand,[5] and also after the healing of the demoniac.[6] When Jesus at the close of his ministry told his disciples of the destruction of the Temple, even they asked what would be the sign of his coming.[7]

When Jesus cleansed the Temple at the beginning of his ministry, the Jews said to him, " 'What sign have you to show us for doing this?' Jesus answered them, 'Destroy this temple, and in three days I will raise it up.' "[8] This was an ideal sign, for he himself was the fulfillment of Temple and sacrificial system. But this miracle that Christ promised was without an Old Testament counterpart, and so it meant nothing to the enemies of Jesus. It

---

[3] See chapter XVII.   [4] John 6:30.   [5] Matt. 16:1.   [6] Matt. 12:38.
[7] Matt. 24:3.   [8] John 2:18–19.

likewise meant nothing to the disciples until after the resurrection!

Christ gave the Jews virtually the same sign, although in different phraseology, when in Matthew 12:38 the Pharisees said, " 'We wish to see a sign from you,' But he answered them, 'An evil and adulterous generation seeks for a sign; but no sign shall be given to it except the sign of the prophet Jonah. For as Jonah was three days and three nights in the belly of the whale, so will the Son of man be three days and three nights in the heart of the earth.' " In Matthew 16:4 he again gives this identical sign of the resurrection.

Christ also dealt with the Jewish logicians, both saints and sinners, by demonstrating to them that they had never come to grips with the truly deep spiritual problems of life. When Jesus talked to Nicodemus about regeneration, the theme was totally beyond him, although Nicodemus was one of the best of the Pharisees.[9] Reread the story of the Samaritan woman at the well and see Christ using the same methodology by again speaking beyond the apprehension of this woman. She, however, was of a different temperament. She reasoned with Christ until she could say the word "Messiah." Then Jesus could reveal himself to her *in person*, and she and her neighbors could be saved.[10]

After the feeding of the five thousand Christ confounded both friend and foe when he said, "No one can come to me unless the Father who sent me draws him; and I will raise him up at the last day."[11] Logic was useless to them then as it is to us now in any approach to knowing the Trinity.

When the Jews insulted Jesus by calling him a Samaritan and insisting that he had a demon, Jesus responded, "I have not a demon; but I honor my Father, and you dishonor me. . . . Truly, truly, I say to you, if any one keeps my word, he will never see death."[12] Then he climaxed that by say-

---

[9] John 3:1–21.   [10] John 4:1–42.   [11] John 6:44.   [12] John 8:49–51

ing, "Your father Abraham rejoiced that he was to see my day; he saw it and was glad."[13] Then beyond all this he staggers them with this remark: "Truly, truly, I say to you, before Abraham was, I am."[14] In the parable of the good shepherd[15] Christ called himself the good shepherd, which instantly identified him with Yahweh, the good shepherd of the Twenty-third Psalm. And to make the identification certain, Christ adds, "I and the Father are one."[16] Again it is the problem of the Trinity. Logic is powerless to deal with the Trinity.

The greatest of all the logical blunders of the scribes and Pharisees was their failure to see the *infinite difference* between "sin" and "sins." And this is still one of the major problems the Church faces today.

The problem of SIN is infinitely deeper than we realize. To get a glimpse at the question of sin, remember that first of all we have a tendency to identify *crime* with *sin.* Crime is only a minor subpoint under sin. Crime can be only against men. *Sin is essentially against God, and even the sins which we commit are not primarily the sins of commission—the times when we knowingly do wrong. The greater sins that we do are the sins of omission—the sins that we never realize are sins!*

Second, remember that man is made in the *image* and *likeness* of God. It is impossible for us to realize how unique we are, how glorious we are, how redeemed we can be! We are made in the image of God himself; and yet, like Adam and Eve, we think we know more than God does. We deify ourselves, hallowing God when it is to our liking, hallowing ourselves when it is our preferred choice. Here is the horror of sin, for sin is the deification of ourselves. Here is the ultimate blasphemy and here is why no man can do anything about sin. In their emphasis on *sins* the scribes and Pharisees had missed all the emphasis on the infinitely greater fact of *sin.*

But at the crucifixion, when God does something about

---

[13] John 8:56.   [14] John 8:58.   [15] John 10:1–18.   [16] John 10:30.

sin, we see the horror of it all, because there is no atonement for sin save God himself! "For God so loved the world that he gave his only Son, that whoever believes in him should not perish but have eternal life."[17] So here is the significance of crime and sin, and here is the significance of redemption. What has happened? Christ has died in our stead and we are now, in the phraseology of Paul, "a new creation." The old is forever past; the new is here. The problem of sin at last is solved and we are saved!

Since the major mistake of the scribes and the Pharisees had been their interest in "sins" instead of sin, they had thus missed the unique significance of the Messiah in the Old Testament. Even on the theme of "sins" the scribes and Pharisees were infinitely below Christ, for it is he who identifies hate with murder, the lustful look with adultery, etc.

But let us never forget that while the scribes and Pharisees became such bitter enemies of Christ that they had to kill him, the common people were hearing him gladly throughout all his ministry. It was the common people who still loved the Old Testament and tried to worship God in the light of his Scripture. They preferred revelation to philosophy.

Now what is the application of all this for today? Let us remember that logic can draw infallible conclusions only when *all the evidence* is available; and let us remember that it is only God who has all the evidence! This is the reason why our prayers should always conclude, "if it be Thy will."

But someone will ask: What about the use of logic in the Christian Church today? Logic has its proper place in the church. It is the best *human* tool that we have for taking the right action. But logic, like a computer, can handle only the information that is put into it. Unlike the days we have been speaking of, we now have the complete

---

[17] John 3:16.

Bible, and it is illuminated by 1900 years of Church history. This complete Bible is the data which the Christian must use in his logical thinking. But even then, if we were to use the whole Bible (and certainly no Christian is blasphemous enough to think that he does this), it would be necessary to obey Christ and say, "If it is Thy will." He himself said it in Gethsemane. Let us likewise say it every day of our lives!

But what about the unbeliever who tries to find God? If in all sincerity he uses logic or any other technique in seeking to find God, and if he is willing to lay down his life to that goal, he will suddenly awake to the fact that God has been seeking him all the time down through the years. And when he finds "that God has found him," all he can do is to echo Thomas and exclaim, "My Lord and my God." Instantly he will give all the credit to God and never cease to wonder why he had not accepted God earlier. Christ speaks of such as these when he talks of those who will "sit at table with Abraham, Isaac, and Jacob in the kingdom of heaven!"[18] Paul was exactly such a logician who was suddenly laid hold on by Christ.

No true Christian will ever ask Athena to share the throne with Jesus the Christ.

---

[18] Matt. 8:11.

XIII

Palm Sunday—King for a Day

WE MUST HASTEN ON to Passion Week, for the Gospel writers give some thirty percent of their text to this one short period. Before Jesus went up to Jerusalem to complete his ministry at the cross, the empty tomb, and the ascension into the clouds above Olivet, he rounded out his preparatory mission at Jericho.

At Jericho, one is reminded that Joshua and Jesus are but different spelling of the same name, which in English means "Yahweh is Salvation." It was at Old Testament Jericho that Joshua (an earlier Jesus) began his conquest of Palestine. It is now at New Testament Jericho, only a short distance from the older site, that Jesus (the last Joshua) begins his final spiritual conquest, not only of Jerusalem and Palestine but of the whole world.

There is an *emphasis on world evangelism* here at Jericho, for it is in this city that Herod the Great had reproduced as much of Augustan Rome as his finances permitted. Indeed, it is the *only* city of its kind that has been excavated to date anywhere east of Italy. The excavations showed a spectacular city laid out on both banks of the Wadi Qelt.[1] Luxury was everywhere. On one bank were

---

[1] The author excavated New Testament Jericho in 1950.

two sets of great buildings whose walls were forty-seven inches thick, and between these massive structures spread a great sunken garden about 360 feet in length. The hillside above the garden was held in place by a retaining wall made up of fifty statuary niches, and in the center of these niches was a semi-circular outdoor theatre with flowering plants between each row of seats. The original flower pots were still in place! In front of the statuary niches and the theatre ran a water-reflecting basin alongside the great sunken garden.

From one of these great buildings a grand stairway climbed up on barrel vaults to a small palatial building which overlooked the whole city. (Some of the original sycamore timbers of this edifice are still in place.) Nearby was another large building with a gymnasium which served as officers' quarters for the army. The ruins of everything that made a great Graeco-Roman city are scattered everywhere along the unexcavated sections of both banks of the stream.

Here too were private villas, and some were finer than those in Pompeii. It was in one of these palatial villas that Zacchaeus entertained Jesus. And remember that Jesus invited himself to this mansion before Zacchaeus was converted! In fact, it was this unique invitation which occasioned the conversion of Zacchaeus. Here near a millionaire's mansion built by a despised tax collector, Christ said, "Today salvation has come to this house, since he also is a son of Abraham. For the Son of man came to seek and to save the lost."[2]

But before Christ came into Herod's Versailles, he had already remembered the poorest and the most unfortunate man in town, a blind man "sitting by the roadside begging." This man anticipated Palm Sunday by crying out, "Jesus, Son of David." "And immediately he received his sight and followed him, glorifying God; and all the people, when they saw it, gave praise to God."[3] It is indeed fitting that such a

---

[2] Luke 19:9–10.   [3] Luke 18:43.

Above: *Excavating Herod's winter capital at Jericho.* Below: *Note the size of the buildings in New Testament Jericho.*

Bethphage (with Transjordan in the background) where the Palm Sunday procession begins.

The modern Palm Sunday procession (top) comes over the Mount of Olives (middle) between the two churches, and crosses the Kidron Valley (bottom of middle photo). Below: the northern half of the Temple area as seen from the Mount of Olives.

tribute by both rich and poor was paid to the work of Jesus just before he went to his crucifixion.

As Jesus drew near to Jerusalem, he told one of the most ominous parables of his ministry—the parable of the pounds.[4] This parable concludes in a verse that should cause abject terror. " 'But as for these enemies of mine, who did not want me to reign over them, bring them here and slay them before me.' "[5] "And when he had said this, he went on ahead, going up to Jerusalem."[6]

The significance of Palm Sunday is seen by the amount of space each evangelist gives to the episode. But before reading their accounts, refresh your memory with the Old Testament history of the Mount of Olives. Because of Absalom's revolt, "David went up the ascent of the Mount of Olives, weeping as he went, barefoot and with his head covered; and all the people who were with him covered their heads, and they went up, weeping as they went."[7] Now David's loyal son, the Messiah, comes back that same road not only as king but as "King of kings and Lord of lords."

Solomon desecrated the extreme southern end of the Mount of Olives by giving it over to the heathen shrines erected to honor the various pagan gods worshiped by the numerous pagan princesses whom he married.[8] These were political alliances, and therefore the religions of the wives had to be respected! From the floor of the Kidron valley in those days one could look to the west and see Solomon's Temple erected in honor of Yahweh. From the same spot one could look eastward to see the Mount of Olives covered with the pagan shrines of Solomon's harem. Solomon's old age was a spiritual tragedy as he fell under the spell of this pagan harem and its still more pagan deities. Christ's reception on Palm Sunday on the Mount of Olives was a national purification of that pagan mountain just across the valley from God's own true sanctuary.

---

[4] Luke 19:11–27.   [5] Luke 19:27.   [6] Luke 19:28.   [7] II Sam. 15:30.
[8] I Kings 11:7, 8.

103

Another Olivet episode may not always be quickly recognized by Bible students. "And the glory of the Lord went up from the midst of the city [Jerusalem], and stood upon the mountain which is on the east side of the city."[9] During Ezekiel's ministry Jerusalem's day of pardon was past. Jerusalem and Yahweh's Temple were about to be destroyed by the Babylonian Nebuchadnezzar. But before the Temple's destruction God departed from his own sanctuary, moved eastward, and stood for a moment on the Mount of Olives!

Now God's own Son comes back from that same Mount of Olives and enters Jerusalem by the same east gate from which the Spirit of God had departed as Ezekiel watched. This Ezekiel passage must have been very vivid in Christ's mind as he made his triumphal entry into Jerusalem. One feature differs. Ezekiel's cherubim were missing,[10] but their place was taken by a multitude who believed in the Messiah, who shouted aloud, "Blessed be the King who comes in the name of the Lord! Peace in heaven and glory in the highest!"[11] When the Pharisees ordered Christ to rebuke his disciples, he replied, "I tell you, if these were silent, the very stones would cry out."[12] If men would not honor their God, the natural world would sing his adoration! Even stones know God better than the most brilliant godless man.

Christ was king for a day. But he was a heartbroken king weeping over Jerusalem, which was soon to be annihilated by the Roman general Titus. "For the days shall come upon you, when your enemies will cast up a bank about you and surround you, and hem you in on every side, and dash you to the ground, you and your children within you, and they will not leave one stone upon another in you; because you did not know the time of your visitation."[13]

Even when he is being acknowledged as "King of kings and Lord of lords," he is still heartbroken that the majority

---

[9] Ezek. 11:23. [10] Ezek. 11:22. [11] Luke 19:38. [12] Luke 19:40.
[13] Luke 19:43–44.

of Israel will reject God's grace and be eternally lost. The archaeologist has watched king after king make his triumphal entry but never a king like this one! May the Lord's Prayer mean more to us as we say, "Thy kingdom come."

When the Pharisees were condemning Christ's triumphal entry, they little realized that they were speaking with prophetic voice: "Look, the world has gone after him."[14] Over twelve centuries earlier another Joshua had conquered Jerusalem, but the Pharisees little realized that this new Joshua's conquest of Jerusalem was at the same time marking the beginning of his conquest of the whole created world.

---

[14] John 12:19.

XIV

Christ Condemns Israel

In the immense courtyard which surrounded the Temple, Christ spent Monday and Tuesday of Passion Week. This courtyard was roughly rectangular, about 1500 feet long and approximately 1000 feet wide. The total circuit of the exterior walls was about a mile. Wide colonnades ran along these walls and gave shelter in times of rain or blazing sun. Here was where the rabbis met their students. At the season of the Passover vast crowds from Palestine and the provinces of the empire would fill the entire courtyard area which was twice as large as the world-famous Acropolis at Athens.

The major archaeological work on the Temple area was done in the last century, and the findings are in the Bible dictionaries and Bible commentaries. Pictures of the area are much better than descriptions, so we are including a number of illustrations. The retaining wall at the southeast corner was 150 feet high during Christ's time. Today the lower half is hidden under the debris of the destruction of Herod's Temple and later Roman buildings. The stones used in this wall were very massive, often running ten to thirty feet in length.

Nothing is left of the sacred Temple itself beneath the present Muslim Dome of the Rock. In this building can be seen a part of the old threshing floor of Araunah the Jebusite, which earlier was most likely the place where Abraham was commanded to offer up Isaac. It was actually an old Canaanite open-air high place, very similar to the one that the author excavated at Bethel.

The Jerusalem Temple was one of the wonders of the ancient world, and the disciples were as enthusiastic about it as any rabbi.[1] But Christ took little interest in the Temple except to cleanse it, for its days were almost finished. The Temple and its sacrificial system were but a part of the plans and specifications of the Messiah. Before the week would be over, the crucifixion and the resurrection would have come to pass and the new dispensation ushered in.

This is why the crucial phrases of Christ's remarks in the Temple courts were directed against the Jewish hierarchy. The importance of the parable of the husbandman who let out his vineyard to tenants can never be overemphasized.[2] In this parable Christ not only accused the Jewish hierarchy of his coming death, but also declared the vineyard to be taken away from Israel and given to others, i.e., the Church. Little did the disciples of Christ or the Jewish hierarchy realize the significance of this worldwide prediction.

Sometime about 1900 B.C. God commissioned Abraham and his descendants to evangelize the world. Throughout two millenniums Israel had occasionally obeyed these orders. But, most of the time she was actually backsliding into paganism or barely holding her own in the faith. Now the Messiah was here! And Israel was about to murder not only her Messiah, but the Savior of the whole world.

With the resurrection of Christ, Israel is no longer God's agent for world redemption; in her place the Church is now commissioned "to make disciples of all nations." The true Israelites who accepted their Messiah constituted the nucleus of this new Church. But when they tried to evan-

---

[1] Mark 13:1. [2] Matt. 21:33–46.

The Muslim "Dome of the Rock" was erected on the site of the Jewish Temple. Note the open courtyard as it was in Christ's time. The Castle Antonia was under the minaret at left of photo above. Below: The Jewish "Wailing Wall" is a section of the old retaining wall of the Temple courtyard.

gelize both Jew and Gentile, it was the Gentiles who came into the Church in mass movements, whereas only a few Jews responded favorably. After the death of Christ the Jewish hierarchy continued their Temple worship until God had given them forty years for repentance; then his Roman legions destroyed that Temple. From that day to this no Jew has been able to worship after the dictates of the Mosaic law.

The Judaism of today is no relative of the Israelite faith of the Old Testament. It is simply an expansion of the same philosophic creed of the Pharisees who crucified Christ. It is a form of Unitarianism. But remember also that the Jew of today is not past redemption. Just as in Old Testament days, any Gentile who accepted Yahweh as his God became a Jew, so now any Jew who accepts Christ as his Messiah can become a Christian. The awful tragedy in all of this, however, is that the Christian Church virtually ignores the evangelism of the Jew just as it ignores its order to evangelize the whole Gentile world.

There were approximately nineteen centuries between the time God commissioned Abraham to evangelize the world and the time Christ removed Israel's commission. Since it is now another nineteen centuries since Christ commissioned the Church, it is high time that we make one last desperate attempt at world evangelism! Why should we, like the Pharisees, busy ourselves with everything under heaven except the one supreme duty of world evangelism? Even today much of the "stuff" that is printed in the name of Christ is as worthless as the Mishnah for the salvation of souls.

Remember the old test that Jesus gave: "By their fruits ye shall know them."[3] Where are the souls of the lost world which Christ entrusted to his Church nineteen centuries ago?

Moving now from earth to heaven, one question put to Jesus by the Sadducees during Passion Week is especially

---

[3] Matt. 7:20, King James Version.

interesting, for in answering it Christ pulled aside the curtain of the future and gave us a momentary glance into heaven. The logical dilemma which the Sadducees presented to Jesus, however, had been intended to show how utterly foolish was *any* doctrine of the future life. It ran like this: There had been seven brothers, and each of them, loyal to the levirate law, had married the same woman and each had died without offspring. Finally the woman died. So, they asked Jesus: "In the resurrection, therefore, to which of the seven will she be wife?" But again Christ reminded the critics that they were in error, since "you know neither the scriptures nor the power of God. For in the resurrection they neither marry nor are given in marriage, but are like angels in heaven."[4]

---

[4] Matt. 22:25–30.

XV

The Last Supper and Gethsemane

JUST AS the Lord had ordered a specific animal for his triumphal entry, so he now ordered the particular accommodations he wished to use for the last Supper.

"And when the hour came, he sat at table, and the apostles with him. And he said to them, 'I have earnestly desired to eat this passover with you before I suffer; for I tell you I shall not eat it until it is fulfilled in the kingdom of God.'" A literal translation of these words would be, "With desire I have desired to eat this passover with you." Christ supremely desired and earnestly looked forward to this event. This meal is so *unique* that Christ will not repeat it "until it is fulfilled in the kingdom of God." He said also of the cup of wine that he would not "drink of the fruit of the vine until the kingdom of God comes."[1] But note that, figuratively speaking, Christ took his cup with him into the garden of Gethsemane. Here is another glimpse into heaven.

During the meal Jesus announced that one of the disciples would betray him. This was in accordance with the

---

[1] Luke 22:14–18.

Messianic plans and specifications: "He who ate my bread has lifted his heel against me."[2] This was, indeed, high treason, for it was this man, whom Christ loved above all of the other disciples, who would betray him! This is symbolized in the oriental idiom of "dipping in the dish"—the symbol by which the host gives honor to his special guest. The honored guest was not Peter who had been the first to call him Messiah, nor John the beloved disciple, but Judas the traitor whom Christ loved best of all!

In commenting on Judas' departure from the table, John adds significantly, "And it was night."[3] Of course, it was night in terms of the hour of the clock, but it was infinitely more. It was night in the heart of Judas, night in the heart of the Jewish hierarchy, night in the heart of all the disciples, and night in the heart of Israel as a covenant people so soon to lose their covenant privileges.

Later, as they were going out to the Mount of Olives, Christ said of all eleven disciples that were with him, "You will all fall away because of me this night; for it is written, 'I will strike the shepherd, and the sheep of the flock will be scattered.' "[4] So when Christ spoke of himself as fulfilling the Scripture—"He was reckoned with transgressors"[5] —it was not only the Jewish hierarchy but even his own disciples who were transgressors. Notice that it was to this group of disciples—every one of whom was to fail him in the crisis hour—to whom Christ said early in the Last Supper, "Truly, truly, I say to you, he who receives any one whom I send receives me; and he who receives me receives him who sent me."[6] As one reads the Gospels carefully he is constantly staggered by the gracious grace of Jesus the Christ!

When the meal was over they sang a hymn.[7] The Passover hymn consisted of Psalms 115–118. Did you ever realize the exalted place that the Psalms held with Jesus?

---

[2] John 13:18; Psa. 41:9.   [3] John 13:30.   [4] Matt. 26:31.
[5] Luke 22:37.   [6] John 13:20.   [7] Matt. 26:30.

When the New Testament was written, snatches of Psalms and hymns were scattered here and there through its pages, but the New Testament never wrote a new praise book to replace the old Psalter! No matter how much we love the Psalms, we can never love them enough. God left them as the praisebook of the Church universal. Certainly we write our own hymns and sing them; and so we should do, for it is one way to praise Christ. But good as these hymns are, they are not Scripture. But when they do reflect Scripture accurately, they can be used of God for any good purpose.

There was mingled joy and sorrow as Christ participated in the Last Supper. After Christ left the upper room he sang his own psalm of triumph over the cross and the grave. "Now is the Son of man glorified, and in him God is glorified; if God is glorified in him, God will also glorify him in himself, and glorify him at once."[8]

But before we leave the Last Supper, note that beginning with the fourteenth chapter of John, Christ is giving a sort of last will and testament—the kind of document that fascinates archaeologists. At this Last Supper Christ had invited himself to a friend's home in Jerusalem. Now Christ invites his immediate disciples and all future followers to his Father's home in heaven! Furthermore, Christ promises that he himself will usher us into the Father's presence! Christ will show us the Father—a privilege no Old Testament saint ever had. "He who has seen me has seen the Father."[9]

Furthermore, "Whatever you ask in my name, I will do it, that the Father may be glorified in the Son." And a second time Christ says, "If you ask anything in my name, I will do it."[10] Then Christ continues, "And I will pray the Father, and he will give you another Counselor, to be with you for ever."[11] And remember that this Holy Spirit whom he gives to us is the third Person of the Trinity! Still continuing his last will and testament, Christ says, "You

---

[8] John 13:31.   [9] John 14:9.   [10] John 14:13–14.   [11] John 14:16.

113

*A thousand-year-old
olive tree in the
Garden of Gethsemane.*

*Armenian foot-washing service
in the Church of St. James.*

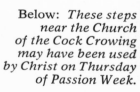

Below: *These steps
near the Church
of the Cock Crowing
may have been used
by Christ on Thursday
of Passion Week.*

will know that I am in my Father, and you in me, and I in you."[12]

Finally he pronounces a benediction: "Peace I leave with you; my peace I give to you; not as the world gives do I give to you. Let not your hearts be troubled, neither let them be afraid."[13] The word "peace" in this passage is the original basic concept of the word. It means reconciliation—restoration to the original state—sin forgiven! In Paul's phraseology, "It is no longer I who live, but Christ who lives in me."[14] And that last will and testament of Jesus Christ covers all future Christians for all time. This will is written in heaven.

GETHSEMANE

The Roman Catholic and the Russian Orthodox churches occupy two different traditional sites for the Garden of Gethsemane, although no one can be certain of the actual site. I recall a vivid service we attended in the garden of the Russian church in memory of Christ's experience in Gethsemane. The Passover moon was exceedingly bright. The tiny olive flowers were in full bloom, and their peculiar fragrance was everywhere. But still more prominent was the rich, heavy smell of the freshly plowed earth between the gnarled olive trees. It was the same fragrance that Christ must have noticed nineteen hundred years ago.

At another time we were taking photographs in the Latin church, which is erected over their traditional site of the spot where Christ prayed in the garden. A Belgian general, his chest ablaze with World War II decorations, was standing erect but with bowed head before the sacred stone. The tears were coursing down his cheeks, and I was aware that here was someone who was sharing the agony of that night with his Christ. It was the most powerful sermon I had ever *seen*.

In the garden Christ prayed three times, saying in substance, "My Father, if it be possible, let this cup pass from

---

[12] John 14:20.   [13] John 14:27.   [14] Gal. 2:20.

me; nevertheless, not as I will, but as thou wilt."[15] "Then he came to the disciples and said to them, 'Are you still sleeping and taking your rest? Behold, the hour is at hand, and the Son of man is betrayed into the hands of sinners.' "[16] When Peter came to defend him against the arresting crowd, Christ said, "Do you think that I cannot appeal to my Father, and he will at once send me more than twelve legions of angels?"[17] Christ could have had at his beck and call more than 60,000 *angels* for his defense, whereas all the legionary Roman soldiers in the whole of the empire from Britain to the Euphrates River were only 300,000 *men*.

When Judas betrayed Christ with a kiss, it could have been the student kissing the rabbi's hand; note that Judas called him "rabbi." But Christ called Judas "friend"—the same title given to the loyal eleven. This was Christ's last attempt to reach the heart of Judas for repentance. Judas fulfilled another Messianic prediction and betrayed Christ with the kiss of allegiance![18] This kiss of loyalty is seen in the episode where Samuel anointed Saul as king of Israel.[19] It was also the kiss of allegiance used in Canaanite worship.[20] Judas was a true Canaanite! Three years with Christ had made no impression on his soul.

---

[15] Matt. 26:39, 42, 44.   [16] Matt. 26:45.   [17] Matt. 26:53.
[18] Matt. 26:54.   [19] I Sam. 10:1.   [20] I Kings 19:18.

XVI

The Cross, His Royal Throne

CHRIST'S TRIAL before Pilate was held either at Herod's former palace near the present Jaffa gate or at the castle Antonia, another major building project of Herod the Great. Part of the remains of the latter are below the Convent of the Flagellation and the Church of the Sisters of Zion. The castle of Antonia is the more likely as it was the key fortress which looked down on the Temple area— the major source of riots in Jerusalem. Pilate and Christ may well have stood on one of the balconies here looking down on the courtyard where the mob was gathered.

This square courtyard seems to have been about 165 feet on a side. The massive stones used in the pavement were about a foot thick and are still in place. You can see where some of them still bear the patterns of the games scratched on them by the Roman soldiers. This may well be "The Pavement" which John mentions as the site of the trial.[1] The whole fortress was approximately 500 feet long and about 250 feet wide. Towers on the corners were said to have been 75 feet high. Cisterns of the old fortress are still in use today. And stones from the catapults of Titus

---

[1] John 19:13.

are still to be seen in places embedded in the castle walls.

Throughout most of the ministry of Christ the leaders of the supreme court of the Jews had already resolved in their individual hearts to kill Jesus. Very early in his ministry the Pharisees and the Herodians had ganged up to destroy Christ.[2] This combination was like a modern collusion of the members of the Birch Society and the Communists. After the healing of the man at the pool of Beth-zatha, "the Jews sought all the more to kill him."[3] The common people knew that their officials were out to murder Jesus, for they said, "Is not this the man whom they seek to kill?"[4] When Jesus was actually brought to trial, every action of the Jewish court was illegal. Therefore let us move on to Christ's trial before Pilate.

We have no Roman sources on Pontius Pilate relative to this trial except a reference by Tacitus to the effect that Jesus was executed by Pontius Pilate in the reign of Tiberius. The emperor must have considered Pilate a good procurator, for he served here from A.D. 26 to A.D. 36. Twelve procurators served a shorter time than Pilate, most of them only a few years. Only one official served longer, and he only one year more. Jewish sources make the following references to Pilate. He had hung blasphemous gilded votive shields in Herod's old palace in Jerusalem, but when the Jews appealed to Rome, Pilate was ordered to remove these offenses. He again offended the Jews by allowing his troops to carry their army standards (the equivalent of our battle flags) into Jerusalem. These standards bore the image of the Roman emperor and thus violated Jewish law. Pilate was also accused of using Temple money to construct an aqueduct which took water from the so-called Pools of Solomon south of Bethlehem to the Temple area in Jerusalem. Sections of this aqueduct with its stone pipes still cemented in place can be seen in Bethlehem. Jewish sources also accused Pilate of breaking all the Ten Commandments.

---

[2] Mark 3:6.   [3] John 5:18.   [4] John 7:25.

In A.D. 36 a Samaritan fanatic claimed that he would uncover the sacred vessels that had been used by Moses on Mt. Gerizim, so armed Samaritans gathered to witness this important event. Pilate called out his troops to disperse them, but he was ruthless in his actions and even executed some of the leading Samaritan officials. For this action he was ordered to Rome by Vitellius, his superior officer, who was the governor of Syria. But the emperor Tiberius died before Pilate arrived in Rome, and we have no later historical data on the procurator.

At the trial of Christ, Pilate himself acted as a normal Roman judge until the very end of the trial, when he was intimidated by the threat of a riot. Contrary to common opinion, Rome did not keep her vast empire in subjection by a massive army. The emperor had major military forces only on the Rhine and the Euphrates frontiers. This left only a very small fraction of his army to police all the rest of the empire which extended from Palestine to Britain. Therefore any questionable gathering that might get out of hand was often put down quickly, ruthlessly, and illegally by all Roman officials.

Peace at any price was the maxim of every minor Roman official; witness Paul's experience at Pisidian Antioch, Iconium, Philippi, Thessalonica, and Ephesus. And remember that Paul was a Roman citizen, perhaps even of equestrian rank (a rank above that of the common people), and to treat a Roman citizen as Paul was treated was a major crime. Note that after Paul's experience at Lystra and Derbe, he retraced his steps through the same cities where he had been driven out, but no one ever touched him again! He must have made known his Roman citizenship after his near lynching at Lystra. At Philippi note how concerned the officials were when they discovered that Paul was a Roman citizen. When Festus, the procurator of Palestine, acted illegally toward Paul, the apostle appealed to Caesar. Although Festus was procurator of Palestine, he had to give in to Paul's request because Paul was a Roman citizen. Christ, however, was a Jew and not a

Roman citizen. Therefore he could make no appeal to Pilate.

Pilate himself four times pronounced Christ innocent, and during the trial he even sent Christ to Herod Antipas to avoid taking unjust action on Jesus.[5] But to Pilate a riot seemed to be at hand, and, as has been mentioned, no Roman official could risk a riot getting out of hand. Pilate was later removed from office for the way he handled the Samaritan riot.

Pilate's wife, like Joseph the husband of Mary, took her dream seriously, and both were correct in doing so.[6] God often works in ways not always appreciated by so-called Bible scholars. All through Scripture God meets the common man on the man's own level, just as he meets the scholar on the scholar's level. God met Pilate's wife on her spiritual level and Paul on his, and he will meet us on ours. Although Pilate did not follow his wife's excellent advice, he did confound the Jews, because he insisted that the cross bear the title, "Jesus of Nazareth, King of the Jews"; and he had it written in three languages (Hebrew, Greek, and Latin) so that everyone could read it.

Crucifixion was used by the Phoenicians and their Carthaginian colonies. Rome then took it over from these North African enemies. In 88 B.C. the Jewish king Alexander Jannaeus put on a mass spectacle of execution when he crucified 800 of his enemies among the Pharisees. At the same time he killed the wives and children of the victims who had to watch from their crosses.

Crucifixion, as a form of capital punishment, put the emphasis on torture, for it was intended to terrify all prospective offenders such as slaves, brigands, and rebels. Even the Roman Cicero commented on the cruelty of crucifixion. Death came slowly since no vital organs were affected, and the victim might hang on the cross as long as nine days before death finally freed him from his torture. The crucified sat on a small wooden "saddle" fastened onto

---

[5] Luke 23:6ff.   [6] Matt. 27:19.

These sections of stone pipe were used in Pilate's aqueduct to bring water from "Solomon's Pools" to the Jerusalem Temple.

Below: The courtyard of the Castle Antonia, where Christ was tried before Pilate.

The good shepherd.

The Castle Antonia lies beneath this area.

the upright timber. His hands were nailed to the cross beam and his feet to the upright timber. The victim's body, cut and bleeding from the scourging which was administered before crucifixion, was then left to the torture of the blazing sun, a burning thirst, and omnipresent flies and insects. The muscles cramped tautly, the nerves of hands and feet agonized, fever mounted, and exhaustion finally released the tortured victim to death.

The Romans made three concessions to the Jews in Palestine. (1) They did not crucify the victim naked. (2) They permitted the Jews to offer a pain-killing drug to the crucified. (Christ refused the myrrh that was offered.) (3) They did not leave the crucified on a cross over the Sabbath.

After the prisoner was sentenced to crucifixion he was scourged; but since Pilate had already scourged Christ as a part of his plan to punish but not to crucify him, Jesus did not undergo a second beating.[7] The victim carried the crossarm to the place of execution.[8] But Christ did not carry it far, for Simon of Cyrene was commandeered to carry the cross.[9] The execution was at Golgotha (The Skull).[10] The most likely site is the Church of the Holy Sepulchre. Recent excavations near that church have demonstrated that this area was outside of the city of Christ's day. Furthermore, since this was the most sacred site in the life of Christ, it must have been remembered by the early Church, as were the sacred sites of the Old Testament.

A normal Roman execution detail consisted of a centurion and four soldiers. Their bonus for this work was the clothing of the victim. Since the seamless robe of Christ was a valuable garment, the soldiers cast lots for it.

All through the Gospel narratives, one is impressed not only by the type of men whom Christ attracted to him but also the occasions of their meetings. Nowhere is this better seen than at the cross. When one of the criminals

---

[7] John 19:1.   [8] John 19:17.   [9] Mark 15:21.   [10] Luke 23:33.

hanging on the adjacent cross confessed his sins and said, "Jesus, remember me when you come in your kingly power," Jesus replied, "Truly, I say to you, today you will be with me in Paradise."[11] Christ was evangelistic even on the cross!

As we read and reread the crucifixion story, we always see the Jews and the Romans busy with the crime of crucifixion. But there is something infinitely more important. In this crucifixion it was Christ himself who *voluntarily laid down his life* as he had said in the parable of the good shepherd: "No one takes it from me, but I lay it down of my own accord. I have power to lay it down, and I have power to take it again."[12] The crucifixion had begun at 9 A.M., and about six hours later Christ cried out, "It is finished."[13] The cross was Christ's *royal throne*. And Christ died at his own appointed time!

But we must not look at the crucifixion by itself. When Christ breathed his last, the curtain of the Temple was torn in two, from top to bottom.[14] The Holy of Holies was now open to all men! Christ, whom the high priest typified, was now ready to take the totality of his Messianic office. The Old Testament Temple was now useless and meaningless, for on Easter dawn the Christ would present the *new temple* of his resurrected body to the world.

"Since it was the day of Preparation, in order to prevent the bodies from remaining on the cross on the sabbath (for that sabbath was a high day), the Jews asked Pilate that their legs might be broken, and that they might be taken away. So the soldiers came and broke the legs of the first, and of the other who had been crucified with him; but when they came to Jesus and saw that he was already dead, they did not break his legs. But one of the soldiers pierced his side with a spear, and at once there came out blood and water."[15]

The minimum time for death by crucifixion was reck-

---

[11] Luke 23:42–43. [12] John 10:18. [13] John 19:30. [14] Matt. 27:51.
[15] John 19:31–34.

oned at thirty-six hours, so the soldier double-checked on Christ by thrusting a spear into his heart. Notice also that "Pilate wondered if he were already dead; and summoning the centurion, he asked him whether he was already dead. And when he learned from the centurion that he was dead, he granted the body to Joseph."[16]

Now we must hurry to "a new tomb where no one had ever been laid."[17]

[16] Mark 15:44–45. Bruce M. Metzger, one of the best New Testament scholars, dates the crucifixion on Friday, April 6 or 7 of the year A.D. 30. (*The New Testament, Its Background, Growth, and Content*, p. 105).

[17] John 19:41.

XVII

The Resurrection

THE BURIAL of Christ is a superb example of love. Shortly before his death he attended a banquet in the home of Simon the leper in Bethany. Here Mary, the sister of Lazarus, anointed Christ with a pound of pure nard which Judas valued as equivalent to the day's wages of three hundred men. In commenting on this gracious act, Christ said, "In pouring this ointment on my body she has done it to prepare me for burial."[1]

The actual burial of Christ was performed by a respected member of that very Sanhedrin that had compelled Pilate to crucify Christ. This Joseph of Arimathea was a "secret disciple" of Christ.[2] But he had bravely voted against the action of the Sanhedrin.[3] He boldly went to Pilate and asked for the body of Jesus. Pilate then checked with the centurion; and when he was assured by him that Christ was dead, "he granted the body to Joseph."[4]

Joseph took the body down from the cross.[5] Nicodemus then joined Joseph, "bringing a mixture of myrrh and aloes, about a hundred pounds' weight. They took the body of Jesus, and bound it in linen cloths with the spices, as is the burial custom of the Jews. Now in the place

---

[1] Matt. 26:12; see also John 12:1-8.   [2] John 19:38.   [3] Luke 23:51.
[4] Mark 15:45.   [5] Mark 15:46.

These tombs date from intertestament times. No doubt Christ saw them many times.

Pilgrims from Europe carry the cross into the Church of the Holy Sepulchre.

This round stone at the mouth of a tomb dates from New Testament times and is like the "stone that was rolled away."

The Garden Tomb (below) dates from Byzantine times, but is the same type as the one described in the Gospels.

where he was crucified there was a garden, and in the garden a new tomb where no one had ever been laid."[6] According to Jewish law Joseph's action was illegal, because the Sanhedrin had two specified places for the burial of their victims. But Christ was honored with a new tomb, and Joseph treated him as a member of his own family. Meanwhile the women were preparing spices to anoint Christ, and they brought them to the tomb at Easter dawn[7]—only to find a Risen Lord!

Several hundred tombs of the first century A.D. have been found near Jerusalem. The "Garden Tomb," although of a later date, is an example of the tomb in which Christ was buried. The actual tomb may be under or near the Church of the Holy Sepulchre. All archaeological evidence now favors this latter site.

The archaeologist knows that the resurrection is unique. Antiquity knew absolutely nothing of the New Testament concept of the resurrection. Even Athens, which had searched the whole world for new ideas, had not known anything like the resurrection until Paul preached it in that city.[8] Indeed, this doctrine was so unique and so significant that Paul, in writing to the Corinthians, said, "If there is no resurrection of the dead, then Christ has not been raised; if Christ has not been raised, then our preaching is in vain and your faith is in vain. . . . If in this life we who are in Christ have only hope, we are of all men most to be pitied."[9]

The Old Testament had seen men brought back to life from the dead. Christ himself had raised the dead—the corpse while it was still in the bed (the daughter of Jairus), the body en route to the cemetery (the widow's son of Nain), and the rotting corpse in the tomb (Lazarus). But these were all brought back to the same earth they had left and to the same totality of environment.

It was different with Elijah, who himself had raised the dead, for he was taken up into heaven in a chariot of fire.[10]

---

[6] John 19:39–41. [7] Mark 16:1, 2. [8] Acts 17:18, 32.
[9] I Cor. 15:13–19. [10] II Kings 2:1ff.

And Peter, James, and John had seen him come down to be with Christ on the Mount of Transfiguration. But even then the meaning of the resurrection was totally unknown until after the bodily resurrection of Jesus the Christ. This is the reason Paul put so much emphasis on the resurrection.

The ancient world never made any real progress in solving the problem of death. The Egyptians were sure they had a solution for it. If you were poor, they dug a hole in the sand and put you in and that was the end of you. But if you were rich or royalty, they believed that by going through certain rites and ceremonies you could arrive into another world, and in that other world you would find yourself in exactly the same situation as you were when you died. That satisfied the Egyptians, but it satisfied nobody else.

The thinking people of the world preferred to go Greek, and the Greeks saw in death only tragedy. Read their literature and look at their tombstones. You will never find any joy that passes all understanding. To them death was a tragedy!

Lazaras did not by himself come back to life; Christ raised Lazarus from the tomb. But Jesus Christ brought *himself* back from the dead.[11] And when he comes back from the dead, *life is entirely different* than when Lazarus came back from the dead. When Jesus comes back, he has a new body, yet it is identical with the one he had before, and so he fellowships and eats with his disciples. But it is a spiritual body; he can suddenly appear in their midst without any warning—even when the doors are locked. Here is Christ, very God of very God and very man of very man; but you are beginning to realize that his deity is now showing forth preeminently. Forty days he stays so that the whole city of Jerusalem can see him. The dead come out of their graves to honor him. He works with his

---

[11] John 2:19; Matt. 26:61.

disciples, and then when the forty days are up, he ascends to the right hand of God the Father.

And then he sends the Holy Spirit—"that other Christ" (which is the literal translation of the Greek in John 14:16)—which he had promised to do. He sends to you "that other Christ," another Comforter and Counselor just like himself, who shall be with you always to lead you into all truth.[12]

At the Last Supper, Christ was trying to get his disciples to understand the resurrection. "Let not your hearts be troubled," he counseled them; "believe in God, believe also in me. In my Father's house are many rooms; if it were not so, would I have told you that I go to prepare a place for you? And when I go and prepare a place for you, I will come again and will take you to myself, that where I am you may be also. And you know the way where I am going."[13] Continuing, he says, "I am the way."[14] This present life for us is but a simple test of a few fleeting days, and then comes life, immortal life!

When I was a little boy my father was working in a shipyard. I used to go down to the shipyard and watch them lay the keel of the ship, rivet on the ribs, put in the bulkheads, put on the plates. Then one day I watched at the launching as that boat left the dry land and went down into the water. Then they finished the work on the ship, and she went out into the sea. That ship was never made to live on dry land! It was built on land, but it was made for the great, great ocean. And so we are built here on land. We build our ship with which we will sail immortal seas. We build it here by the grace of God and the help of Jesus Christ and the indwelling of the Holy Spirit. And then at death "the Pilot" comes on board and takes us to his own country—the blessed country.

The resurrection is so unique that it is memorialized by an entirely new kind of Sabbath, the Christian Sabbath.

---

[12] John 14:15–17, 26; 15:26; 16:13–15.   [13] John 14:1-4.
[14] John 14:6.

The Old Testament Sabbath was the memorial of the creation of the natural world; it was so significant that God blessed it *and* sanctified it (man was only blessed). Now the new Sabbath is the memorial of the *new* creation, of the *new* world in which the Christian is infinitely more unique than Adam. The believer is now an adopted child of God the Father and a citizen of heaven. These two concepts are far too deep for us to comprehend. But we, like Paul, can appreciate in some degree our absolute uniqueness in that *it is no longer we who live, but Christ who lives in us.*

The resurrection and its new Sabbath memorial are so unique that the Sabbath is the *only* holy day in the New Testament calendar. The Old Testament had a yearly calendar with many holy days in addition to the Sabbath. But in the New Testament there is no yearly calendar. Now there is only a weekly calendar. Sabbath worship in the new dispensation must never cease to emphasize the future sinless life in the Father's home, which is ours through the atoning work of Jesus the Christ.

132

XVIII

Christ Ascends to Heaven

FORTY DAYS marked the period of Christ's temptation at the beginning of his ministry. Now at the close of that ministry came another unique forty-day period.[1] During this time Christ completed the education of his disciples, so that they in turn could teach believers of all future generations how to meet the temptations of Satan as Christ himself had done.

But this postgraduate course, which the disciples took under their risen Lord, was different from their original three-year study period with them. They now saw Christ with *all* the emphasis upon his deity and they *worshiped him*.[2] Bruce M. Metzger has well phrased it. "Moreover, the experiences during those six weeks assisted the disciples to think of their Lord as absent and yet living; as invisible and yet near them; as risen to a new life and yet retaining the same nature which they had loved; as exalted but still the same (compare Heb. 13:8)."[3] Luke summarizes Christ's postgraduate course as follows: " 'These are

---

[1] Acts 1:3.   [2] Matt. 28:17.
[3] *The New Testament, Its Background, Growth, and Content*, pp. 130–131.

my words which I spoke to you, while I was still with you, that everything written about me in the law of Moses and the prophets and the psalms must be fulfilled.' Then he opened their minds to understand the scriptures, and said to them, 'Thus it is written, that the Christ should suffer and on the third day rise from the dead, and that repentance and forgiveness of sins should be preached in his name to all nations, beginning from Jerusalem. You are witnesses of these things.' "[4]

Jesus had come into his earthly life so quietly that men thought of him as just another Jewish baby. But when the Christ left earth and ascended into heaven the disciples were already worshiping him. Then in the light of the ascension and the later gift of the Holy Spirit the disciples again reevaluated everything that Christ had taught them in his three-year ministry. John could summarize it in this unique phraseology: "There are also many other things which Jesus did; were every one of them to be written, I suppose that the world itself could not contain the books that would be written."[5]

But before Christ ascended to the right hand of the father, he gave the disciples their final assignment. "Go therefore and make disciples of all nations, baptizing them in the name of the Father and of the Son and of the Holy Spirit, teaching them to observe all that I have commanded you; and lo, I am with you always, to the close of the age."[6]

But we must cross over into the book of the Acts to get the last episode of the ascension. Christ again pledged his disciples the gift of the Holy Spirit and again commanded them to evangelize the world. "And when he had said this, as they were looking on, he was lifted up, and a cloud took him out of their sight. And while they were gazing into heaven as he went, behold, two men stood by them in white robes, and said, 'Men of Galilee, why do you stand looking into heaven? This Jesus, who was taken up from you into

---

[4] Luke 24:44–48.   [5] John 21:25.   [6] Matt. 28:19–20.

heaven, will come in the same way as you saw him go into heaven.' "[7]

The Savior-teacher will return on the same clouds of heaven to give his students their final examination on world evangelism.

[7] Acts 1:9–11.

XIX

The Miracle of Christ and Miracles

"UNTO *his own* he came and yet *his own* received him not."[1] This is a literal translation of verse 11 in the prologue to John's Gospel. There is a play on the words "his own." The first occurrence is neuter gender, the second is masculine.

When Christ came with his miracle-working power, everything in the natural world obeyed him as its Creator. He spoke to the storm-tossed Sea of Galilee and it was instantly quiet. He turned water into wine. He spoke to the barren fig tree and it withered. The hogs of the Gerasenes were at his bidding and rushed to destruction in the sea. Every malady of the physical human body responded to the command of Christ. The blind saw, the paralytic walked, the leper was cleansed. Every disease was conquered. Even the dead obeyed him. Lazarus came forth from the tomb.

Everything in the natural world obeyed Christ whether it was in the domain of matter or in the domain of life. It was only the immortal souls of men (made in the image and likeness of God) that refused to accept Christ. The

---

[1] John 1:11.

problem of "miracle" then falls into two categories: (1) the problem of the miracle of Christ himself, and (2) the problem of the miracle in the natural world of matter and life. Let us study the first, for this is where we have contemporary data.

The Christian of today is saved in exactly the same way as were the disciples whom we have been studying. Paul, who like ourselves was not of the group that followed Christ personally, said, "I know whom I have believed." The exact meaning of "know" is to "learn by personal experience"—not by hearsay or report or by study, but by *personal experience.* And the full extent of this personal experience with Christ is expressed by Paul in these words: "It is no longer I who live, but Christ who lives in me."[2] Furthermore, this converted Pharisee could speak like this because of his deep conviction of sin, for he says of himself even late in his ministry, "I am the foremost of sinners."[3]

The sincere experienced Christian of today knows exactly the same experience as the New Testament Christians who worked personally with Christ. "Jesus Christ is the same yesterday and today and for ever."[4] The miracle of all miracles is Christ himself—very God of very God. Yet he became very man of very man and was born of the virgin Mary. And as the God-man he died on the cross and made redemption for a lost world.

Christ is known by faith and faith alone. And that faith is a personal experience with Jesus the Christ. Paul was one of the most brilliant Pharisaic scholars in Jerusalem and highly honored by the Jerusalem hierarchy with diplomatic duties of life and death abroad. But when Paul met Jesus his Christ en route to Damascus, Paul's personal experience with Christ was conversion. Then after conversion Paul's brilliant mind was given still more brilliancy by the Holy Spirit, and Paul today ranks as one of the greatest scholars in all of history. Notice how much of your New Testament is Pauline.

The archaeologist knows the religious leaders of antiq-

---

[2] Gal. 2:20.   [3] I Tim. 1:15.   [4] Heb. 13:8.

uity and of later times such as Mohammed, but they have no real relationship to Christ. Christ is unique! Let us use an analogy. Compare the anthropoid ape with man in each and every factor of man's personality and work, and you are forced to recognize the absolute uniqueness of man whether you are an evolutionist or a creationist. Even more so, Christ is infinitely unique.

The more I work as an archaeologist with truly great scholars in any related field, the more I see men who are Christians first and world scholars afterwards! The truly great scholar is the one who knows that human personality is the greatest of all earth's problems. But he also knows that his obedience to Jesus the Christ will alone enable him to solve these problems of human personality which include himself, mankind, and the natural world. Paul is the patron saint of all great scholars. But Christ is the only one whom all men can worship and obey!

The next outstanding miracle after Christ himself is the Bible. In the New Testament we have the code book by which we know Christ via the personal tutorship of the Holy Spirit. The Bible—the totality of it—is the greatest book in the world. By its fruits you know it. No book is even competitor to it in worldwide translation. No book is competitor to it in any sense!

When the Jews took the Old Testament without the New Testament, they found themselves with a book that was lifeless—a dead fossil. It was the Christians and not the Jews who turned the world upsidedown; and the Christians did it using both the Old Testament and the New Testament as a single volume. Mohammed took what he wanted of both Testaments, but his Muslim followers made their conquest with the sword and not with the Koran. And today the Muslim, like Rip Van Winkle, has waked up to a new world where his Koran is useless.

One question remains. What is the relationship of the New Testament to the Old Testament? What is this unity? Here is the best analogy that I know in answer to this query. Modern science became uniquely new with the discovery of atomic physics. For the first time in the history of scientific study it opened the way to an understanding of matter and life. In the same way Christ himself opens for us the ultimate satisfying interpretation of the book he himself used as his Bible, i.e., the Old Testament. Furthermore, he gave us the Holy Spirit whom he promised would lead us into all truth.

To know the miracle of the Bible at its best, you must read it under the tutorship of the Holy Spirit. The clergy are helpful; Bible commentaries are of assistance; but it is from the Holy Spirit alone that we can get the *totality of truth in personal experience.* Therefore, whenever you read the Bible, always read it with a prayer that the Holy Spirit may lead you into the deep things of God.

The Bible itself is its own best defender and evangelist. A pastor friend of mine was working with an outstanding scholar in one of the most modern fields of science trying to lead the man to Christ. The pastor told this man to sit down with the Bible just as he would with one of his best scientific treatises and give the Bible the same honest judgment and appreciation that he gave science. It was only a little later than an honest scientist accepted Christ as his personal Savior. (But do not forget that meanwhile the pastor had also been in intercessory prayer for this scholar.)

Coming now to the problem of miracles in the natural world such as changing water to wine, stilling the sea, raising the dead, etc., let us remember that the Creator is master of his own universe. I am reminded of a story told me by one of my professors. He had written his first book, and the publisher was going out of his way to please his new author. The publisher told the author that he would give him the first bound copy of his book. The professor replied, "How can there be a first copy, since you are doing all your work on the book by *machinery?*" The publisher replied, "But professor, we are printing and binding your copy by *hand.*"

This is a parable of how Christ works. He works

through the natural laws which he established at creation's dawn, and their uniformity is one of our greatest blessings. But the Creator Christ can also work "by hand," without the benefit of natural laws. Cannot THE MIRACLE work miracles?

But strangest of all, Christ is willing to share his power with his believers, for at the Last Supper he said, "Truly, truly, I say to you, he who believes in me will also do the works that I do; and greater works than these will he do, because I go to the Father."[5]   We will not do works that are identical with Christ's, but works which are related to his.   One of his major tasks was healing the physical body. But he could cure only a few of the sick folk of Palestine, and all the millions of the rest of the ancient world went untouched.   Now Christ works by opening the doors of science and teaching the physician, and that knowledge can go to the ends of the earth.   Not that all physicians are Christians, just as in Christ's time those who did miracles in his name were not all Christians.   But the true physician, if he has genuine concern for the sick, shows forth the love and work of Christ.

Christ's more important work was to bring men to God. Again, he could reach only so many souls in a twenty-four-hour day, and his ministry at the longest estimate was only three years.   And again, only Palestine and adjacent countries saw his personal ministry.   But at the same Last Supper he promised the Holy Spirit to his disciples, and now every Christian can be a soul-winner.   This is why Christ commanded us, "Go therefore and make disciples of all nations, baptizing them in the name of the Father and of the Son and of the Holy Spirit, teaching them to observe all that I have commanded you; and lo, I am with you always, to the close of the age."[6]   Saved men are among the most important miracles of the miraculous Christ!

---

[5] John 14:12.   [6] Matt. 28:19–20.

XX

Luke's Postscript

LUKE was the only one of the evangelists who made a two-volume work out of the ministry of Christ! It was he alone who saw that the earthly ministry and the heavenly ministry of Christ were one and inseparable. So Luke's book of the Acts "takes up the amazing story where the Gospels drop it and it tells us of His session at the right hand of the Majesty on high; of His administration of the Kingdom of God from thence; of His personal superintendence of every movement of His church in its lofty mission to the world; and of His control of the great forces both of the visible and invisible world. We learn from it that angels, devils, men, and even inanimate things are now under the sway of Him whose purposes of grace are being accomplished in His mediatorial government of the universe."[1]

Within ten years of the close of Luke's second volume on the Gospels, Jerusalem and its Temple had been destroyed and the Old Testament sacrificial ritual gone forever. Within less than twenty-five years after the close of Acts every book in the New Testament had been written and the Scripture canon closed.

---

[1] William G. Moorehead, *Outline Studies in Acts, Romans, I & II Corinthians, Galatians and Ephesians* (Old Tappan, N.J.: Fleming H. Revell Co., 1902), p. 9.

It is impossible to overestimate Luke's significant use of a two-volume work to tell the full gospel story. Even so, it is impossible to overemphasize John's brief postscript to his Gospel: "But there are also many other things which Jesus did; were every one of them to be written, I suppose that the world itself could not contain the books that would be written."[2]

---

[2] John 21:25.

The text of this book was set in the new type face Aster by Kingsport Press, Kingsport, Tennessee. Hadriano was used for the chapter titles combined with Hadriano Stone Cut.